**Workbook**

*Books published in PSM:*

**PSM ∅A**   Flow charts  Number i  Fractions i  Angles i  Measurement i
Statistics i  Number ii  Angles ii
**PSM ∅B**   Measurement ii  Sets  Number iii  Fractions ii  Symmetry
Measurement iii  Starting Grids  Statistics ii
**PSM ∅ Workbook**
**PSM ∅ Teacher's Guide**
**PSM ∅ Visual Aids Package**


**PSM 1a**   Sets I  Symmetry  Fractions I  Measurement I
**PSM 1b**   Fractions II  Graphs and Functions I  Angles and Parallels  Statistics I
**PSM 1c**   Graphs and Functions II  Fractions III  Primes and Indices  Bearings
**PSM 1d**   Measurement II  Substitution  Locus  Fractions IV
**PSM 1 Workbook**
**PSM 1 Teacher's Guide**


**PSM 2e**   Directed Numbers  Vectors I  Constructions  Brackets and Equations I
**PSM 2f**   Ratio  Travel Graphs  Sets II  Moving Shapes
**PSM 2g**   Brackets and Equations II  Estimation and Approximation
Angles and Shape  Statistics II
**PSM 2h**   Percentage I  Pythagoras  Number Bases  Circles
**PSM 2 Workbook**
**PSM 2 Teacher's Guide**


**PSM 3i, j**   Vectors II  Sets III  Solids  Brackets and Equations III  Calculation Aids
Factors and Indices  Percentage II  Scale Drawing
**PSM 3k, l**   Brackets and Equations IV  Isometries  Graphs and Equations  Matrices I
Simultaneous Equations  Measurement III  Inequalities  Matrices II
**PSM 3 Workbook**
**PSM 3/S Teacher's Guide**

# PSM Ø

**Workbook**

Joint Editors
**Shirley Lee and Donald Stagg**

**Stanley Thornes (Publishers) Ltd**

First published in 1987 by:

Stanley Thornes (Publishers) Ltd
Old Station Drive
Leckhampton
CHELTENHAM GL53 0DN
England

British Library Cataloguing in Publication Data

Lee, Shirley
    PSM 0.
    Workbook
    1. Mathematics—Examinations, questions, etc
    I. Title     II. Stagg, Donald
    510'.76     QA43

    ISBN 0-85950-584-7

Typeset by KEYTEC, Bridport, Dorset, England
Printed and bound in Great Britain at The Bath Press, Avon

# CONTENTS

Acknowledgements   vii

1. Flow Charts   1

2. Number i   13

3. Fractions i   21

4. Angles i   30

5. Measurement i   38

6. Statistics i   47

7. Number ii   59

8. Angles ii   69

9. Measurement ii   79

10. Sets   89

11. Number iii   97

12. Fractions ii   105

13. Symmetry   115

14. Measurement iii   121

15. Starting Grids   130

16. Statistics ii   139

N.B.   Throughout this book * indicates a question where some practical activity can be involved.

# ACKNOWLEDGEMENTS

PSM Ø was written by a group of experienced teachers.

Shirley Lee and Donald Stagg (Joint Editors), Nigel Buckle, John Eadie, David Hanson, Mark Harvey, Nigel Kinloch, Martin Kneath and Jasper Selwyn

would like to thank John Hersee for his encouragement and support, and the following schools for their cooperation over testing material:

Downsend Lodge
Newland House School
Long Close School
Castle Court School
Rowan Preparatory School

Aberlour House
Surbiton High Junior School
Great Bookham County Middle School
Claygate County Middle School

# 1. Flow Charts

If a photocopier is available, copies may be taken of the diagram* on p.4.

*Note: Copyright is waived on this diagram only.

## PRACTICE 1 (AB)

Take the boxes in the order in which they are written.

The arrows tell you which way to go.

**1**

*Speedily* fill in the empty boxes in these flow charts, with suitable words:

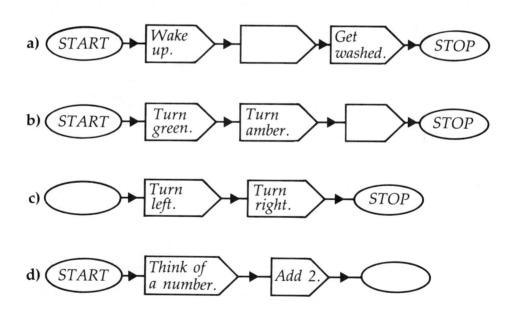

a) START → Wake up. → ☐ → Get washed. → STOP

b) START → Turn green. → Turn amber. → ☐ → STOP

c) ◯ → Turn left. → Turn right. → STOP

d) START → Think of a number. → Add 2. → ◯

**e)** In answering these questions:

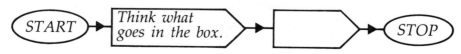

START → Think what goes in the box. → ☐ → STOP

1

**2**

Here are ten flow chart boxes. Write down the boxes in the correct order as a flow chart.

( STOP )    ( START )

| Hold toothbrush under tap. |

| Remove top of the toothpaste tube. |

| Move toothbrush up and down. |

| Take toothbrush out of mouth. |

| Put toothbrush in mouth. |

| Squeeze toothpaste tube. |

| Hold toothbrush under toothpaste tube. |

| Spit out toothpaste. |

 **3**

Imagine yourself on a floor covered with large square carpet tiles.

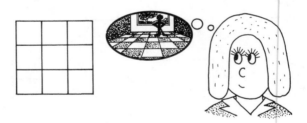

There are just two instructions which you can use:

> Move one square forwards.

> Turn right.

To make life easier, we will show these two instructions as follows:

This means: 'move one square forwards'.

This means: 'turn right'.

2

In each of these questions, you can use the boxes as many times as you wish!

*For example:* Move two squares forwards and two to the right.

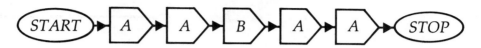

Make your own flow charts, like the one above, for these:

**a)** One square forwards and three to the right.

**b)** Two squares forwards.

**c)** One square forwards and one to the right.

**4**

Here is a nearly completed flow chart for making a large banana sandwich.

Fill in the two empty boxes.

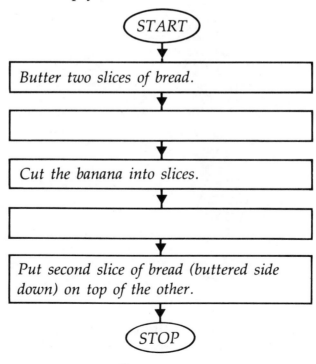

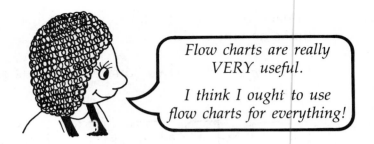

**\*5**

Tom is just going to climb a mountain, but first he must get his feet into good condition.

Unfortunately Emma dropped his flow chart!

Write the boxes in the correct order (or cut up a photocopy and paste them in the correct order).

# PRACTICE 2 (C)

When using a calculator, it is very important to press the buttons in the correct order.

 **1**

*Speedily* work out, using your calculator:

**a)** $57 + 85 + 39$          **b)** $200 - 74 - 38$

**c)** $57 \times 14$          **d)** $338 \div 13$

**e)** $9 \times 7 \times 8$          **f)** $45 + 94 - 37$

 **2**

This flow chart shows how to multiply by 9:

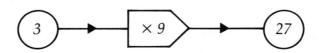

In this example, when 3 is 'fed in ', 27 'comes out'.

What numbers would come out if the following were fed in to this flow chart?

**a)** 2          **b)** 8          **c)** 7

**d)** 6          **e)** 40

What numbers were fed in if the following came out?

**f)** 81          **g)** 72          **h)** 108

**i)** 9          **j)** 45

5

**3**

This flow chart has had ink spilled on it!

a) Suggest *two* possible 'labels' for the box.

b) If 4 is fed into this flow chart then 6 comes out.

 Which of your two 'labels' in (a) must be the correct one?

What will come out if the following are fed in?

c) 10                    d) 46                    e) 89

f) 7                     g) 109

What numbers would have been fed in if the following came out?

h) 101                   i) 70                    j) 34

k) 2                     l) 1001

 **4**

Tom has a flow chart which changes 3 into 9 and 5 into 13. He was showing it to Libby when she unfortunately dropped it!

**a)** Rearrange the boxes so that the flow chart works again properly.

**b)** What would come out if 7 was fed in?

 **\*5**

Here are 6 keys to press on a calculator:

| 4 | | 3 | | + | | × | | 5 | | = |

Write down the order in which you should press these keys (once each only) to get the result 32.

# SUMMARY

 **1**

*Speedily* fill in the empty boxes in these flow charts:

**a)** 4 ➤ × 2 ➤ ➤ 10

**b)**
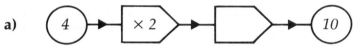

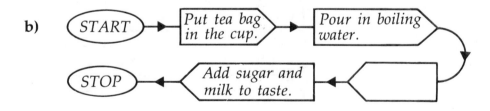

**c)** ○ ➤ × 2 ➤ + 3 ➤ 11

**d)** Writing a letter O on a piece of paper:

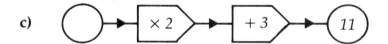

**e)** 3 ➤ ➤ × 2 ➤ + 3 ➤ 11

7

**2**

Here are 7 boxes. Arrange them in a suitable order to make a flow chart:

| Unwrap end of chocobar. | ( STOP ) | Give money to shopkeeper. |

| Chew. | Bite off a piece. |

| Put end of chocobar in mouth. | ( START ) |

 **3**

Here are the stages in Emma's special method for making a cup of tea for Dr Ivel:

| Give three anticlockwise stirs. |

| Pour about 3 ml of milk into cup. |

| Give six clockwise stirs. |

| Put two spoonfuls sugar into cup. |

| Pour tea into cup. |

**a)** In which order do you think she does these?

Arrange these boxes as a suitable flow chart so that Libby can use it to make tea for Dr Ivel (who is *very* fussy about his tea!) while Emma is away visiting the dentist.

**b)** Arrange the same boxes into a different order which could also produce a good cup of tea!

**c)**

Hamish has decided that he can do it just as well as any girl, but Dr Ivel is not too impressed!

Hamish did *everything* that Emma does, but got the order wrong.

Draw another flow chart to show how Hamish could have done it!

 **4**

Libby presses these keys in order on her calculator:

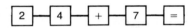

**a)** What answer will she get?

What would she get if she pressed them in the following orders?

**b)** | 2 |—| + |—| 4 |—| 7 |—| = |

**c)** | 2 |—| + |—| 7 |—| 4 |—| = |

**d)** | 2 |—| 7 |—| + |—| 4 |—| = |

**e)** | 7 |—| 2 |—| + |—| 4 |—| = |

**f)** | 7 |—| + |—| 4 |—| 2 |—| = |

**g)** | 4 |—| 2 |—| + |—| 7 |—| = |

 ***5**

Tom has pressed these keys on his calculator:

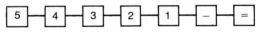

9

He pressed them once each, but he can't remember in which order he pressed them!

His calculator shows the result 469 .

In which order do you think he pressed the keys?

# ALLSORTS

**1**

HAMISH    CHOCOLATE    EMMA    KNOWS    LOVES

a) Write these words in a sensible order.

b) Try to find another suitable order!

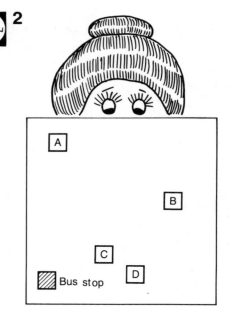

**2**

Miss Layshun is going shopping. She must buy 1 kg sugar from the grocer's shop A, a new shopping bag from the store B, 5 kg potatoes from the greengrocer's shop C, and she must get some money from the bank D.

She travels to and from town by bus.

Plan Miss Layshun's best route as a flow chart.

**3**

Hamish loves chocolate things. Make a flow chart to show him how to cook this:

# CHILDREN'S CHOCOLATE FACES

100 g self-raising flour
1 × 15 ml spoon cocoa
    powder
pinch of salt
100 g margarine
100 g caster sugar
2 eggs, lightly beaten

Place 15 paper cake cases on a baking sheet. Sieve the flour, cocoa and salt. Cream the margarine and sugar until light and fluffy. Beat in the eggs, and one tablespoon of the flour and cocoa. Fold in the remaining flour and cocoa. Divide the mixture between the cake cases. Bake in a moderately hot oven for 15–20 minutes (Oven: 190 °C). Allow to cool.

 **4**

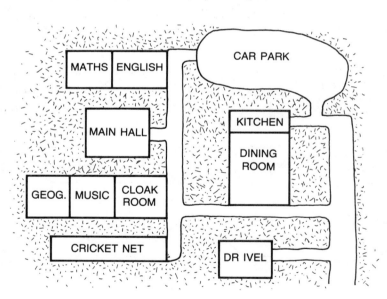

Hamish has to be in the main hall at 0900 when he arrives at school by car. Then he has Geography, English, Music and Mathematics. Next it is lunch, but afterwards he must see Dr Ivel on the way to practise cricket in the nets.

Draw a flow chart showing Hamish's movements! (He is allowed to visit the cloakroom.)

11

**5**

Look at these boxes:

$L$ > means 'turn left'. $R$ > means 'turn right'.

$O$ > means 'turn the opposite way'.

Also remember the 4 points of the compass

In the questions which follow, if you *always* start facing North, in which direction will you be facing when you stop?

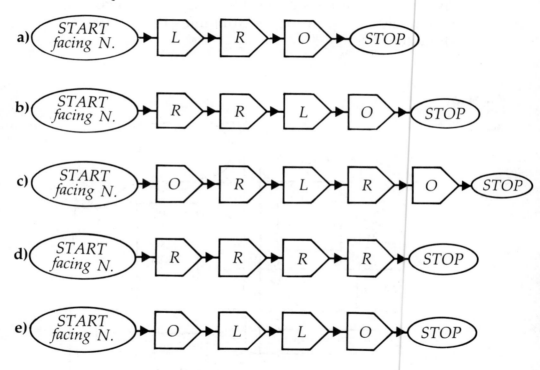

a) START facing N. ► L ► R ► O ► STOP

b) START facing N. ► R ► R ► L ► O ► STOP

c) START facing N. ► O ► R ► L ► R ► O ► STOP

d) START facing N. ► R ► R ► R ► R ► STOP

e) START facing N. ► O ► L ► L ► O ► STOP

# 2. Number i

We use a decimal system of counting, base ten. 3<u>6</u>5 means 3 hundreds, 6 tens, 5 units. The 6 underlined has the value sixty (60).

**1**

*Speedily* work out the value of each digit underlined.

Put column headings to help you if you need them.

HTU
For example, 1 <u>2</u> 4 → 2 tens = 20

a) 3<u>4</u>0

b) 1<u>1</u>20

c) 79<u>9</u>

d) 1<u>8</u>645

e) <u>2</u>902

f) 1<u>1</u>10

g) 77<u>7</u>7

h) <u>7</u>0070

i) 1010<u>1</u>

j) <u>1</u>00 000

13

**2**

Mr Rolls is counting his stock of Mars bars. He has 5 boxes which each have 100 bars in them and he has 16 packets which have 10 bars in each packet. How many bars has he altogether?

**3**

Emma collected 30 conkers. She gave 12 to Tom and 9 to Fatima. How many did she keep for herself?

**4**

Jonathan is collecting comics. He has 14 Beanos, 7 Roy of the Rovers and 11 others. How many more does he need to collect to have 40 comics altogether?

**5**

210 cartons of milk are delivered to Upstart Lodge School each day. There are 10 cartons needed for the staff. Jonathan takes a tray of milk to 10 classrooms with the same number of milk cartons on each tray. How many cartons are there on each tray? (Use your unequal sharing flow chart to help you, from Book A, p.28.)

# PRACTICE 2 (BC)

To work out an approximate answer, round up or down to the nearest 10.

For example, 77 is 80 to the nearest 10.

 **1**

*Speedily* round the following up or down to the nearest 10 p.

a) 99p

b) 52p

c) 29p

d) £1.01

e) £1.99

f) £41.09

g) £999.99

h) £89.05

i) 21p

j) 19p + 19p + 19p

 **2**

Work out the approximate cost of this shopping then add up the amounts to find the approximate total.

For example, 31p × 3 is approximately 30p × 3 = 90p.

a) 6 books at £1.95 each.

b) 3 kg apples at 95p for 1 kg.

c) 4 records at £4.78 each.

d) 12 packets of crisps at 19p each.

e) 9 chocolate biscuits at 11p each.

f) 10 grapefruits at 21p each.

g) Find the approximate total.

15

**3**

At the school fête Hamish was helping to count up the takings at the tuck stall. Work out how much money was collected altogether.

60 coins worth 2p each
3 coins worth 50p each
23 coins worth 10p each
10 coins worth 5p each
15 coins worth 20p each
2 coins worth £1 each

60 lots of 2p...

**4**

**a)** Share 10 jam tarts between Tom and Jonathan so that Jonathan has 2 more than Tom.

**b)** Mrs Haddock, the cook, has rolled out a long piece of dough. It is 1 metre long! She cuts off 16 cm to begin with and cuts the rest into 12 equal pieces to make apple turnovers. What length will each of the 12 pieces be?

**5**

Tom was doing his Christmas shopping. Look at part (a) below: Tom gave the shopkeeper 50p to pay for a bar of chocolate which cost 31p. His change was 19p. Copy (a), (b), (c), (d) and (e) and fill in the spaces. If possible use a quick way to work out each of the answers.

|  | *Tom gave:* | *The cost is:* | *Tom's change:* |
|---|---|---|---|
| **a)** | 50p | 31p | ? |
| **b)** | £1 | 69p | ? |
| **c)** | 40p | ? | 18p |
| **d)** | £1 | 48p | ? |
| **e)** | 60p | ? | 41p |

**f)** How much did Tom spend altogether?

16

# SUMMARY

 **1**

*Speedily* work out the following. Work out the brackets
first—in your head if possible.

For example, $(12 - 2) \div 5$
$$= \quad 10 \div 5$$
$$= \quad 2$$

**a)** $(10 - 2) \div 4$       **b)** $(26 - 4) \div 2$

**c)** $(100 - 10) \div 10$       **d)** $(50 - 10) \div 4$

**e)** $(12 + 24) \div 3$       **f)** $(10 + 5) - 5$

**g)** $(100 + 50) - 100$       **h)** $(100 - 100) \times 2$

**i)** $(60 \times 2) \div 10$       **j)** $(1 \times 1 \times 1) \div 1$

 **2**

Libby, Tom and Morag go tadpoling. They catch
42 tadpoles altogether and decide to share them equally.
Tom says that as it was his net and his idea, he should
have 6 more than the others.

**a)** How many tadpoles did Morag and Libby have each?

**b)** How many did Tom have?

17

**3**

Emma has to buy 1 kg apples and 2 kg pears. The apples cost 85p for a kg and the pears 65p for a kg.

a) How much did she pay altogether?

b) Emma gave the shopkeeper £2.50. She received 3 coins as change. What value were the coins she was given in her change?

**4**

All the children in the school are to be given a packet of potato crisps at the school Christmas party. To estimate about how many packets will be needed, Miss Layshun looked at the list of numbers in each class and made her estimate by rounding up or down.

a) Look at the numbers below and work out the *estimated* number of packets required by rounding the numbers up or down to the nearest 10 to help you.

| | | |
|---|---|---|
| Class | 1 | 19 |
| Class | 2 | 22 |
| Class | 3 | 26 |
| Class | 4 | 24 |
| Class | 5 | 18 |
| Class | 6 | 21 |
| Class | 7 | 20 |
| Class | 8 | 19 |
| Class | 9 | 14 |
| Class | 10 | 18 |

b) Work out the *exact* number of packets of crisps needed.

c) Work out the difference between your answers to (a) and (b).

**\*5**

Using either counters or by drawing a picture show how you would share 60p between Tom and Jonathan so that Jonathan has 10p more then Tom.

# ALLSORTS

**1**

Fatima's auntie gave her a box containing 100 Smarties. She decides to share them with three of her friends, but feels that she must have only 16 Smarties herself.

**a)** How many Smarties will Fatima's friends each have if they all have the same amount?

**b)** How many less does Fatima have?

**2**

Use these column headings if necessary to help you and write down the following numbers in figures.

TTH    TH    H    T    U

**a)** Three thousand and eleven

**b)** Sixteen thousand two hundred

**c)** Twenty-six ones

**d)** Forty-nine tens

**e)** Four hundred and twenty

**3**

Libby was doing some shopping for her mother. She used an easy method to work out in her head the cost of what she was buying as she went along.

Now work out the exact cost of each item. (Remember first to round up or down to make the working out easier.)

**a)** 3 packets of biscuits at 39p each packet    =

**b)** 4 boxes of sweets at 81p each box    =

**c)** 7 cans of drink at 24p each can    =

**d)** 2 books at £1.98 each book    =

**e)** 5 bags of sugar at 52p each bag    =

**f)** How much did Libby spend altogether?

(It was very heavy to carry all that shopping home!)

 **4**

**a)** Tom has mixed up his shopping list and the prices he paid. He's been trying to work out exactly what he spent in each shop and has just a few gaps to fill in. Copy what Tom has written and fill in the missing prices.

Spent

Shop 1 Eggs 59p, Cheese ?    £1.39

Shop 2 Magazine ?, Newspaper 20p    £0.91

Shop 3 Cabbage 40p, Potatoes 38p £0.78

**b)** Tom's gran gave him £4 to pay for the shopping. How much change did he give her?

 **\*5**

Find out more about the ways people have counted in the past. There may be a book to help you in the library.

*I've made a tally stick so that both Miss Layshun and I can remember that she owes me 3 Mars bars!*

*I'm going to make an abacus.*

# 3. Fractions i

$$\text{Fraction} = \frac{\text{NUMERATOR}}{\text{DENOMINATOR}}, \text{ for example } \frac{3}{4}$$

 **1**

*Speedily* write down whether the 15 is the numerator or the denominator in each of the following fractions:

a) $\frac{4}{15}$  b) $\frac{10}{15}$  c) $\frac{15}{16}$  d) $\frac{8}{15}$  e) $\frac{15}{32}$

f) $\frac{15}{1001}$  g) $\frac{1}{15}$  h) $\frac{18}{15}$  i) $\frac{11}{15}$  j) $\frac{15}{8}$

 **2**

Write these statements as fractions:

**a)** 3 sweets from a bag of 7.

**b)** 15 marks out of a possible total of 25.

**c)** 4 pieces out of a cake which has been cut into 9 pieces.

**d)** 18 sandwiches eaten from a plate of 30.

 **3**

On squared paper draw a rectangle 3 squares across and 4 squares down.

21

**a)** Shade $\frac{3}{4}$ of the rectangle.

**b)** What fraction is unshaded?

**c)** How many squares are shaded?

**d)** How many squares are unshaded?

 **4**

Mrs Haddock has been given a lovely new pie dish which she uses to serve 6 people. She has served out the pieces which are dotted.

**a)** What fraction of the pie has she served?

**b)** What fraction is left?

 **5**

Write down whether the following are proper fractions, improper fractions or mixed numbers:

**a)** $\frac{7}{3}$     **b)** $2\frac{1}{3}$     **c)** $\frac{3}{7}$     **d)** $\frac{5}{13}$

**e)** $\frac{14}{9}$     **f)** $1\frac{2}{3}$     **g)** $\frac{16}{15}$     **h)** $\frac{27}{29}$

**i)** $5\frac{17}{18}$

Any fraction with the same numerator and denominator makes up one whole number.

For example, $\frac{6}{6} = 1$

**1**

*Speedily* copy and complete:

**a)** $1 = \frac{9}{?}$ 

**b)** $\frac{10}{?} = 1$ 

**c)** $\frac{?}{13} = 1$

**d)** $1 = \frac{?}{101}$ 

**e)** $1 = \frac{87}{?}$ 

**f)** $\frac{4}{?} = 1$

**g)** $\frac{19}{?} = 1$ 

**h)** $1 = \frac{?}{5}$ 

**i)** $1 = \frac{?}{11}$

**j)** $\frac{18}{18} = \frac{9}{?}$

Equivalent fractions have the same value. If you multiply the numerator and denominator by the *same number*, the value of the fraction stays the same.

For example, $\frac{1(\times 2)}{2(\times 2)} = \frac{2}{4}$, so $\frac{1}{2}$ and $\frac{2}{4}$ are equivalent fractions;

$\frac{2(\times 3)}{3(\times 3)} = \frac{6}{9}$, so are $\frac{2}{3}$ and $\frac{6}{9}$.

**2**

Copy and complete these, multiplying the numerator and denominator of the *first* fraction by the same number, to make the *second* fraction equivalent to it.

**a)** $\frac{2}{3} = \frac{}{6}$ 

**b)** $\frac{3}{4} = \frac{}{12}$ 

**c)** $\frac{2}{3} = \frac{8}{}$ 

**d)** $\frac{3}{5} = \frac{}{15}$

**e)** $\frac{1}{7} = \frac{2}{\phantom{x}}$  **f)** $\frac{3}{7} = \frac{\phantom{x}}{21}$  **g)** $\frac{5}{6} = \frac{\phantom{x}}{24}$  **h)** $\frac{3}{8} = \frac{6}{\phantom{x}}$

**i)** $\frac{5}{8} = \frac{\phantom{x}}{24}$  **j)** $\frac{7}{8} = \frac{49}{\phantom{x}}$

 **3**

Draw a circle and divide it into four equal parts.

**a)** Shade in three of the parts.

**b)** What fraction of the circle have you shaded?

**c)** Divide each of the four parts into half.

**d)** How many parts altogether now?

**e)** What fraction of the circle is now shaded?

**f)** Copy and complete: $\frac{3}{4} = \frac{?}{8}$.

 **4**

Copy and complete the following sets of equivalent fractions:

**a)** $\frac{2}{3} = \frac{?}{6} = \frac{?}{18} = \frac{60}{?}$

**b)** $\frac{2}{3} = \frac{6}{?} = \frac{24}{?} = \frac{?}{360}$

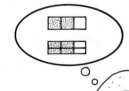

 **5**

**a)** Change $\frac{3}{4}$ into sixteenths.

**b)** Change $\frac{2}{7}$ into fourteenths.

24

c) Write $\frac{45}{60}$ in its simplest form.
   (Look on p.59 of 'Fractions i' if you have forgotten how to find the simplest form.)

d) Change $\frac{3}{5}$ into fifteenths.

e) Change $\frac{16}{28}$ into sevenths.

f) Write $\frac{8}{16}$ in its simplest form.

## SUMMARY

 **1**

*Speedily* write down the fraction of the figure which is shaded in each of these drawings, writing your answers in their simplest form:

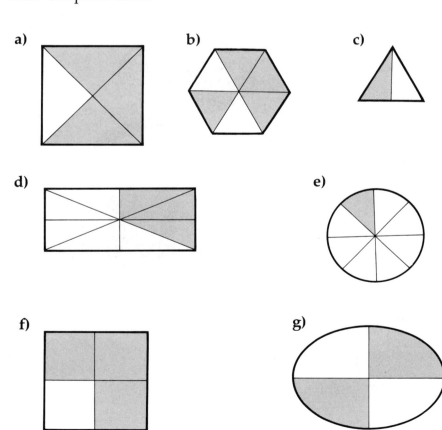

a)

b)

c)

d)

e)

f)

g)

**h)**

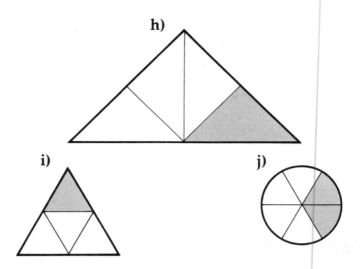

**i)**

**j)**

 **2**

If a farmer has 180 sheep and sells 36 of them, what fraction of his sheep will he have left?
(Write your answer in its simplest form.)

 **3**

What is the equivalent fraction to:

a) $\frac{1}{2}$ which has a denominator of 8?

b) $\frac{1}{4}$ which has a denominator of 12?

c) $\frac{1}{5}$ which has a denominator of 15?

**d)** $\frac{5}{7}$ which has a denominator of 14?

**e)** $\frac{4}{5}$ which has a denominator of 20?

 **4**

Jonathan's mother gives him
a birthday cake which looks
like this.

Jonathan, Libby and Hamish
have a piece each, the
shaded pieces.

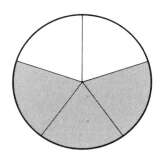

**a)** What fraction of the cake will be left?

**b)** How could you divide the two remaining pieces of
cake, so that each of the three children receive equal
shares?
(Draw a picture to help you.)

 **5**

Write these statements as fractions, giving your answers in
simplest form.

**a)** 24p spent from 80p pocket money.

**b)** 10 minutes out of a lesson of 40 minutes.

**c)** 4 cm of ribbon cut from a length of 9 cm.

**d)** 19 postage stamps from a collection of 100.

# ALLSORTS

**1**

Here is a rectangle, measuring 6 cm by 4 cm, with a shaded square inside it.

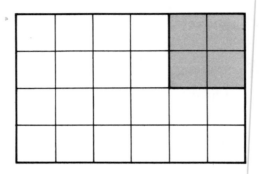

The shaded square measures 2 cm by 2 cm.

**a)** How many centimetre squares are there in the whole shape?

**b)** How many centimetre squares are there in the shaded square?

**c)** What fraction of the large rectangle is shaded?

**d)** Write this fraction in its simplest form.

**e)** Write a similar fraction for the unshaded part of the large rectangle.

**f)** Draw a 6 cm by 4 cm rectangle and use it to show that $\frac{6}{24} = \frac{1}{4}$.

**2**

Last night 240 people attended the farewell concert of the Haggis All Stars Pipe Band. 80 were men, 144 were women and the rest were children.

**a)** How many children were there?

**b)** What fraction of the people at the concert were men?

**c)** What fraction were women?

**d)** What fraction were children?

**3**

Tom spent 40 p on bus fares, 50 p on sweets and he gave 10 p to a woman collecting for retired mathematics teachers.

**a)** What fraction of the total did he spend on each?

**b)** Draw a diagram to show this.

**4**

Remembering that $\frac{12}{24}$ is larger than $\frac{9}{24}$, follow these instructions:

**a)** Change each of these fractions so that they have a denominator of 24:

$$\frac{5}{8}, \frac{13}{24}, \frac{1}{2}, \frac{2}{3}, \frac{7}{12}$$

**b)** Arrange the fractions, with denominator 24, in order of size with the smallest first.

**c)** Now write the original list of fractions in (a), that is $\frac{5}{8}$, $\frac{13}{24}$, etc., in order of size with the smallest first.

**5**

'Give your brother the larger half of the cake.'

Explain what is wrong with this instruction.

29

# 4. Angles i

**1**

*Speedily* write down which of these angles are: acute, right, obtuse or reflex.

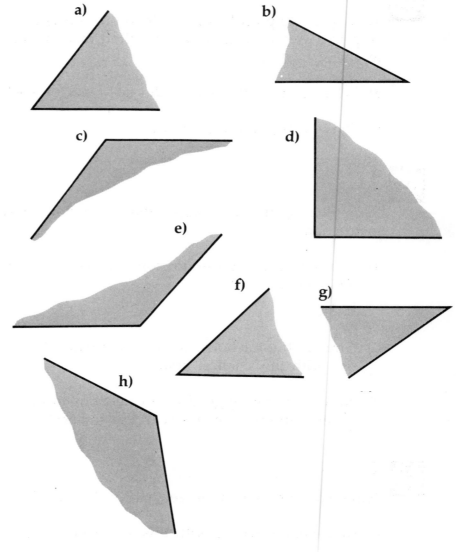

a)

b)

c)

d)

e)

f)

g)

h)

**2**

What kind of angle is turned through by the following?

**a)** A book is lying closed on the desk; its cover is opened to point to the ceiling.

**b)** A soldier who does an 'about turn'.

**c)** The cover of an open book when you close it.

**d)** A man facing west who turns to the east.

 **3**

Make a flow chart to show what you do if you stand up to face the front of your classroom and turn round a half-turn.

 **4**

Write down the names (e.g. obtuse) we give to the following angles:

**a)** 51°　　　　　　**b)** 139°　　　　　　**c)** 247°

**d)** $89\frac{1}{2}°$　　　　**e)** 92°

 **5**

Copy and complete:

**a)** An acute angle is ..................................... than 90°.

**b)** An angle of exactly 90° is called a .................... angle.

**c)** An obtuse angle is ........ than 90° but ........ than 180°.

**d)** A straight angle is exactly .......................................°

**e)** An angle of more than 180°, but less than 360°, is called
.................................................................................

# PRACTICE 2 (C)

 **1**

*Speedily* estimate the number of degrees in the following angles. Write your answers to the nearest 10°.

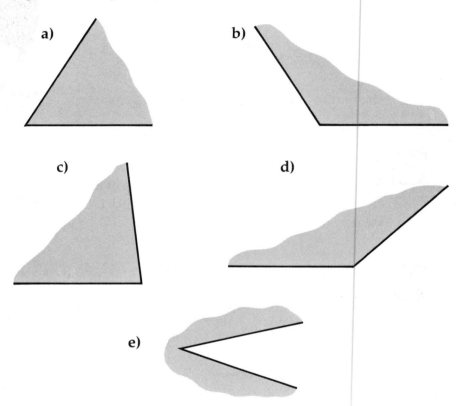

a)

b)

c)

d)

e)

 **2**

Use your triangular protractor to measure the following angles to the nearest 10°.

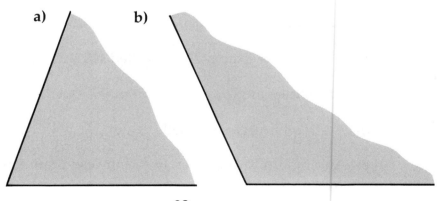

a)

b)

c)

d)

e)

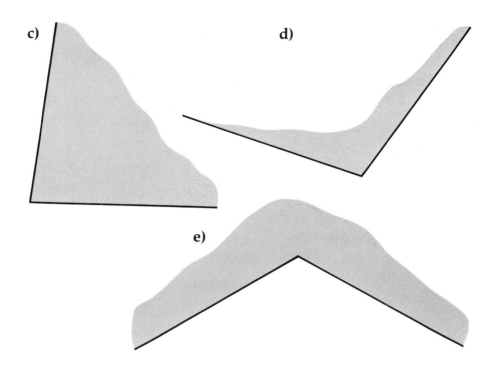

 **3**

Draw neat diagrams to show you know and understand the meaning of the following words about angles:

**a)** acute

**b)** obtuse

**c)** right

**d)** reflex

 **4**

Now measure the angles you drew for question 3, and write your answers to the nearest 10°.

# SUMMARY

If one object makes a square corner with another, we say 'it is at right angles to it'.
For example, two walls of a room which are next to each other are at right angles to each other.

33

**1**

Make a list of about 5 pairs of things in your classroom which are at right angles to each other.

 **2**

The minute hand is pointing to 12 on a clock. What kind of angle does it move through to point to:

**a)** 20 past      **b)** $\frac{1}{2}$ past      **c)** 45 minutes past

**d)** 55 minutes past      **e)** $\frac{1}{4}$ past      **f)** 25 minutes to

 **3**

**a)** 51° is an example of an acute angle. Write down 5 more examples of acute angles.

**b)** 124° is an example of an obtuse angle. Write down 5 more examples of obtuse angles.

**c)** 227° is an example of a reflex angle. Write down 5 more examples of reflex angles.

 **4**

Measure the following angles to the nearest 10° and say what kind of angle each is:

**a)** 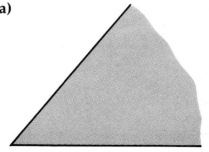      **b)**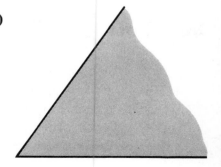

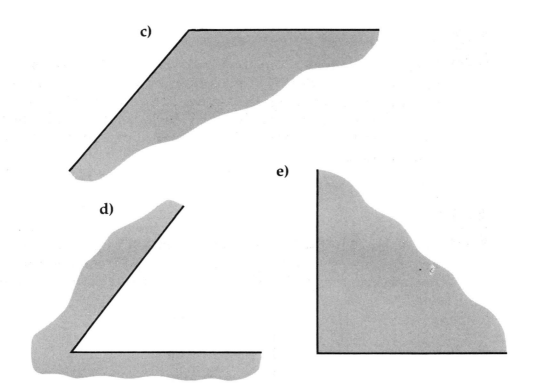

c)

e)

d)

**\*5**

Make an interesting design by joining different kinds of angles together, for example 1 right angle joined to 3 acute angles joined to 2 obtuse angles joined to 1 reflex angle. Make up your own.

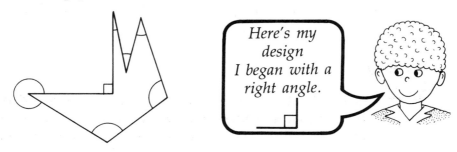

*Here's my design I began with a right angle.*

# ALLSORTS

**1**

Write down all the numbers you can think of which divide exactly into 360; put them in order, smallest first. Be careful—you should find 24 of them.

**\*2**

The Earth revolves about the Sun once every $365\frac{1}{4}$ days; this was the old idea of a revolution. Nowadays, we think of a revolution as being 360°. Why do you think 360 is a more convenient number than $365\frac{1}{4}$? Discuss this with your teacher, or a friend, and write a sentence or two to explain your thinking.

 **\*3**

The diagram below, made with a square, can be used to measure angles. Use a square of tracing paper to copy the diagram accurately. All of the angles marked with a dot are equal.

Now write sentences to answer these questions.

**a)** How many angles are there?

**b)** If they all add up to 360°, what size is each one?

 **\*4**

You need 2 tracings of the square above. Instead of using your protractor, think of ways to measure the angles below using the *angles* of the squares you have just traced.

**a)**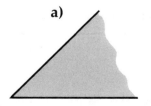

**b)**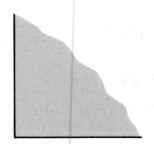

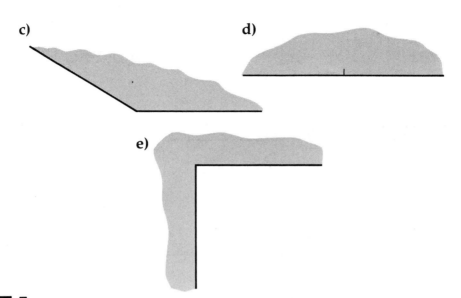

c)

d)

e)

**5**

Tom and Hamish have a race. Tom starts from point P, Hamish starts from Q. Tom runs round the square track, while Hamish runs round the circular track. They both finish where they started. Which of the sentences below do you think is true? Copy your choice and write a short sentence to explain it.

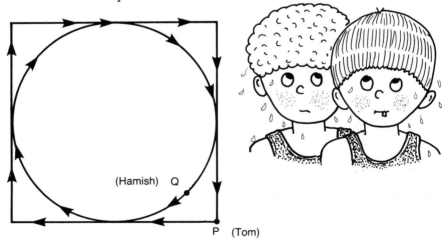

(Hamish) Q

P (Tom)

*Possible answers:*

a) Tom and Hamish have both turned the same number of degrees.

b) Tom has turned more degrees than Hamish.

c) Hamish has turned more degrees than Tom.

# 5. Measurement i

10 mm = 1 cm

100 cm = 1 metre

**1**

*Speedily* work out which is bigger:

a) 25 mm or 26 cm    b) 3 cm 7 mm or 28 mm

c) 1 cm or 100 mm    d) 10 cm or 101 mm

e) 13 mm or 1 cm    f) 1 m or 170 cm

**2**

Emma's atlas is quite a big book.
She finds that it is 3 spans across and 4 spans long. Each
span is about 12 cm.
About how wide and how long is her atlas?

**3**

a) Measure the lines AB, AC, AD, DC, CB on the diagram
and write down their lengths.

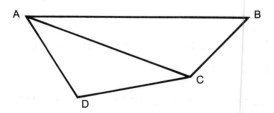

b) Which line is the longest?

38

**c)** Which line is the shortest?

**d)** What is the difference between the length of the longest line and the shortest line?

 **4**

Use a sharp pencil for this question and do it carefully. Use the squares of your book to help you draw perfect right angles.

Draw triangles of the sizes given below, then measure the third side of each.

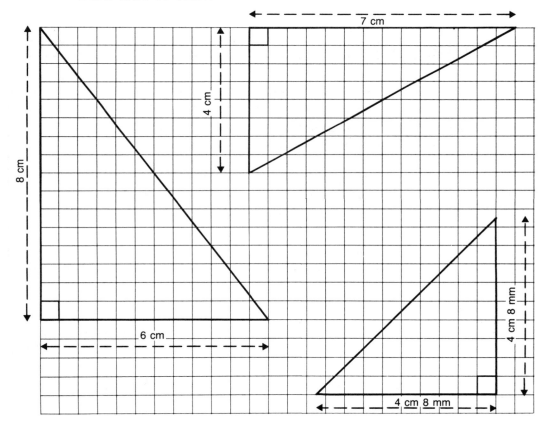

 **\*5**

Stand against the wall, without your shoes on, and ask a friend to mark your height carefully.
Measure this in cm and mm.

Ask your teacher first of course, and use a flat book to find the exact point on the wall to mark.

mark

Use this to guess how tall your friends are and even how tall your teacher is.

Try to measure them too, after you have written down your guess, to see how good you are at estimating.

# PRACTICE 2 (C)

When changing one unit into another always ask yourself the questions below to help.
For example, to change 60 cm to mm:

(1) Will there be more or less?—(more mm)
(2) How many times more or less?—(10 times more; $10 \times 60 = 600$ mm)

Answer: 600 mm

 **1**

*Speedily* copy these questions out, putting the right number in place of the ?.

a)   50 mm = ? cm                 b)   4 m   = ? cm

c)   10 m   = ? mm                 d)   1 mm = ? cm

e)  600 mm = ?cm                  f)   45 cm   = ? mm

*Perimeter* is the distance all the way round the edge of a shape.

**2**

Emma's dictionary is smaller than her atlas. It measures about 16 cm by 23 cm.

**a)** Draw a freehand sketch of the dictionary and then work out its perimeter in cm.

**b)** More careful measurement shows the lengths to be 15 cm 8 mm and 23 cm 4 mm.
What is the more carefully measured perimeter? Answer in cm and mm.

 **3**

Look back to Practice 1.

Use your diagrams of the triangles in question 4, to work out the perimeters of the three triangles.

*Draw the triangles again to help you if you want.*

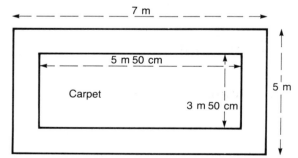 **4**

The diagram below shows a carpet on the floor of a dining room. It is not drawn to scale.

7 m

5 m 50 cm

Carpet

3 m 50 cm

5 m

**a)** What is the perimeter of the *room*?

**b)** What is the perimeter of the *carpet*?

41

**\*5**

The straight on a school running track is usually 60 m or 100 m long. If your school has a running track, find out its exact length from a teacher.

**a)** Estimate (guess) how many paces you would take to walk along the straight.

**b)** Pace it out properly and count your paces.

**c)** How long is each of your paces?

**d)** How many paces would you take to go 400 m?

**e)** How many would you take to go 1000 m?

# SUMMARY

 **1**

*Speedily* work out:

Write in mm:     **a)** 43 cm          **b)** 1 m

                 **c)** 250 cm         **d)** 22 cm

Write in cm:     **e)** 1 m 42 cm      **f)** 10 mm

                 **g)** 4 m 71 cm      **h)** 5 m 6 cm

42

**2**

A ball of garden twine is 27 m long.
It is cut into 6 equal lengths.
How long is each piece?
Answer in m and cm.

 ***3**

Find the three largest books on the shelves of your room.
Measure the width and the length of one page of each
book putting your results in a table like the one below.
Work out the perimeter of each book.
Use cm and mm and be as careful as you can.

|  | Width | | Length | | Perimeter | |
|---|---|---|---|---|---|---|
|  | cm | mm | cm | mm | cm | mm |
| Book 1 |  |  |  |  |  |  |
| Book 2 |  |  |  |  |  |  |
| Book 3 |  |  |  |  |  |  |

 ***4**

**a)** Measure a 2p piece, across its width. The width is
called the diameter.

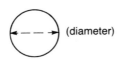

(diameter)

**b)** Do the same for a 5p piece and complete the table
below.

| Coin | 1p | 2p | 5p | 10p |
|---|---|---|---|---|
| Width | 2 cm |  |  | 2 cm 8 mm |

43

**c)** Jonathan decided to see how many pennies would make a row of coins one metre long, that is 100 cm long.
As each 1p coin is 2 cm wide Jonathan could see he needed . . .

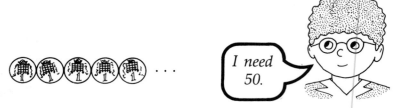

Work out how many 2p, 5p and 10p coins you would need to make one metre.

 **\*5**

**a)** Find out the length and width of your school hockey or football pitch.

**b)** Guess how many paces you would take if you paced it out in the ordinary way.

**c)** Now run quite fast and count these paces—they are probably longer so there will be fewer.

**d)** Work out the perimeter and put all your results in a neat table.

|  | Metres | Walking paces | Running paces |
|---|---|---|---|
| Length |  |  |  |
| Width |  |  |  |
| Perimeter |  |  |  |

# ALLSORTS

 **1**

Hamish ties up 7 parcels for his friends, all exactly the same.
Each parcel uses up 75 cm of string.

How much string has he used:

**a)** in cm?

**b)** in m and cm?

 **\*2**

Find a milk bottle and a piece of string about 2 m long.

**a)** Wrap the string round the milk bottle five times and measure carefully exactly how much string you used to do this. Answer in cm.

Divide this answer by 5 to find out the perimeter or *circumference* of the milk bottle.

**b)** Do the same experiment on another round object, like a tin of beans or a vase.
Make sure you keep the string tight.
Why is it better to wrap it round several times instead of just once?

**c)** Push a bicycle along to find out the circumference of the wheels.
Mark a point on the tyre with chalk and go several turns (five or six) to make it as accurate as you can, giving your answer in m and cm.

**3**

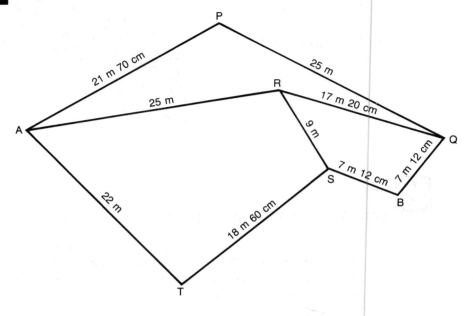

There are four ways of getting from A to B which use exactly three stages.

(Don't bother about ones which use more than three stages.)

One of these is:

|  | | |
|---|---|---|
| AP | 21 m 70 cm |
| PQ | 25 m |
| QB | 7 m 12 cm |
| Total distance | 53 m 82 cm |

**a)** Work out the total distances for the other 3 routes.

**b)** Which is the shortest route?

**c)** Which is the longest route?

46

# 6. Statistics i

## PRACTICE 1 (A/B)

**1**

This pictogram shows how much pocket money some of Emma's friends have each week. ◯ represents 20p (so △ represents 10p)

| Tom | ◯ ◯ ◯ ◯ |
|---|---|
| Hamish | ◯ ◯ ◯ ◯ ◯ |
| Libby | ◯ ◯ ◯ ◯ △ |
| Emma | ◯ ◯ ◯ |
| Jean–Pierre | ◯ ◯ △ |

*Speedily* work out these answers:

**a)** How much does Tom have?

**b)** How much does Jean-Pierre have?

**c)** How much more does Tom have than Jean-Pierre?

**d)** How much does Emma have?

**e)** How much less does Emma have than Hamish?

**f)** How much do they have altogether?

**g)** If ◯ represented 15p how much would Hamish have?

**h)** If ◯ represented 15p how much would Tom have?

**i)** If ◯ represented 30p how much would Libby have?

Remember to use the flow chart on p.95 of 'Statistics i' to help you to draw the pictogram in question 2.

**2**

The children were asked by Tom which of the following foods they liked best for breakfast. Below are the numbers of children who choose each item.

Sausage:   5       Baked beans: 4
Fried egg:  2       Mushrooms:  3

Draw a pictogram to represent this information; use the symbol 人 to represent one child.

 **3**

Hamish asked his friends which make of car they liked best.

| | | | |
|---|---|---|---|
| Tom: | BMW | Jean-Pierre: | BMW |
| Hamish: | Ford | Jonathan: | Ford |
| Emma: | Mercedes | Morag: | Vauxhall |
| Libby: | Vauxhall | | |

Draw a bar chart to show this information but use 'Statistics i' Book A, to help you (pp.98–100).

 **4**

### Books Hamish's Friends like Reading

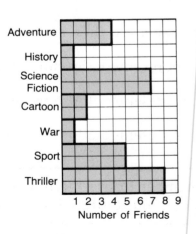

48

Use the bar chart to answer these questions:

a) Which are the most popular books?

b) Which are the least popular?

c) How many friends like books on sport?

d) How many more friends like thrillers better than books about sport?

e) How many friends were asked altogether?

 *5

Write down the names of 6 famous television personalities.

Show your list to 15 friends and ask them who they like best.

When you have collected all the information represent it:

a) as a pictogram.

b) as a bar chart.

# PRACTICE 2 (C)

 1

*Speedily* work out the following.

If a pie chart represented 20 people what fraction of the circle would show:

a) 10 people?

b) 5 people?

c) 1 person?

d) 2 people?

e) 17 people?

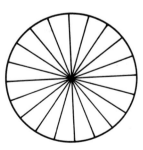

If a pie chart represented 60 people how many people would be represented by:

**f)** $\frac{1}{4}$ of the pie?

**g)** $\frac{7}{60}$ of the pie?

**h)** $\frac{1}{2}$ of the pie?

**i)** $\frac{3}{4}$ of the pie?

**j)** $\frac{1}{3}$ of the pie?

 **2**

Emma's pie chart shows the colour of car that her teachers have.

**Car Colours**

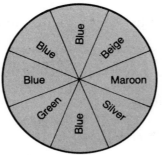

**a)** Which colour is the most popular?

**b)** How many other colours are there?

**c)** How many cars are there altogether?

**d)** What fraction of all the cars are blue?

 **\*3**

Jonathan asked his friends to name their favourite hobby. These are their replies:

| | | | |
|---|---|---|---|
| Cycling: | 4 | Swimming: | 2 |
| Reading: | 3 | Cubs/brownies: | 2 |
| Computer games: | 4 | Stamp collecting: | 1 |

50

**a)** By following the flow chart below, draw a pie chart showing this information.

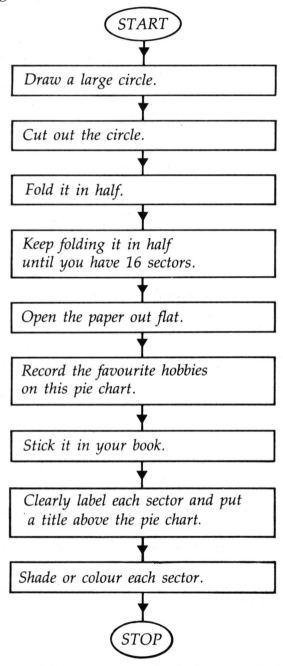

START

Draw a large circle.

Cut out the circle.

Fold it in half.

Keep folding it in half until you have 16 sectors.

Open the paper out flat.

Record the favourite hobbies on this pie chart.

Stick it in your book.

Clearly label each sector and put a title above the pie chart.

Shade or colour each sector.

STOP

**b)** How many children were asked about their favourite hobby?

**c)** What fraction of Jonathan's friends liked either cycling or computer games?

**d)** What fraction of Jonathan's friends liked cubs/brownies?

51

**4**

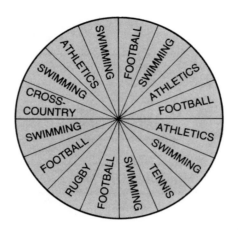

**a)** What is a suitable title for this pie chart?

**b)** How many people chose swimming?

**c)** What is the least popular sport of those shown?

**d)** What is the most popular sport of those shown?

**e)** How many more people chose swimming than football?

**f)** How many fewer chose rugby than chose athletics?

**g)** What fraction of the people chose athletics?

**h)** What fraction of all the people chose tennis?

**i)** How many people were asked about their favourite sport?

**\*5**

Choose a survey you would like to carry out. Ask 16 people. When you have all the information record it:

**a)** as a pictogram;

**b)** as a bar chart;

**c)** as a pie chart.

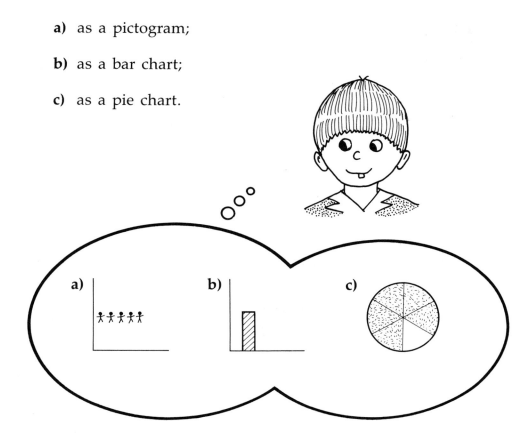

# SUMMARY

**1**

*Speedily* work out how many cartons of milk are delivered in these roads altogether when ☐ represents 10 cartons, ⊓ represents 5 cartons.

| | |
|---|---|
| High Street | ☐ ☐ ☐ ☐ ☐ |
| Low Road | ☐ ⊓ |
| River Avenue | ⊓ |
| Ferry Drive | ☐ ☐ ☐ ⊓ |
| Long Street | ☐ ☐ ☐ ☐ ☐ ☐ ☐ ☐ |

**2**

Look carefully at this bar chart and answer the questions below.

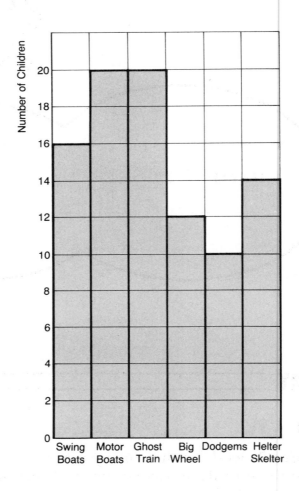

**Children's Favourite Rides at the Fair**

a) How many children are represented by one square?

b) Which rides are twice as popular as the dodgems?

c) If 6 girls like the dodgems best how many boys prefer them?

d) How many children are represented on this bar chart altogether?

**\*3**

Use the information from question 2 and draw a pictogram. Make up your own symbol and use it to represent 2 children.

**4**

**The Corner Shop's Takings for a Week in July**

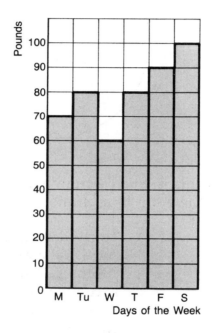

a) Write down how much the shop takes on each day.

b) Work out the week's total takings.

**\*5**

Use the bar chart in question 4 to help you make up a bar chart of your own to show the shop's takings for a week in December. As the weather was very bad the Corner Shop only took half as much money in December, so think carefully as you draw your bar chart.

55

# ALLSORTS

 *1

Trace this pie chart which has been divided into 12 sectors. It will be used to show the months of the year.

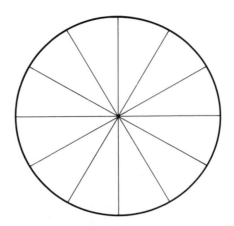

**a)** Read this rhyme carefully which tells you how many days there are in each month:

> Thirty days has September,
> April, June and November.
> All the rest have 31
> Excepting February alone
> Which has 28 days clear
> And 29 in each leap year.

**b)** Shade in the fraction of the pie which represents the months with 30 days.

**c)** Leave blank the fraction of the pie which represents the months with 31 days.

**d)** Put dots in the sector which represents February.

**e)** Label the sectors of your pie chart 30 days, 31 days, 28 days.

**f)** Make up a suitable title.

**\*2**

**a)** Make a list of 10 common British birds.
(Look up the names of some if necessary.)

**b)** Ask 10 friends to give you the names of 5 common British birds.

**c)** Each time a friend says the name of a bird you have on your list, put a tick.

**d)** Make a bar chart to show which birds are the most well-known among your friends.

 **\*3**

Do the same as you did in question 2 but this time use common British trees.

 **4**

Miss Layshun set an hour-long test which Libby thought was far too long. She spent $\frac{1}{4}$ hour fiddling with her pen and cartridge and all the other things in her pencil case. 30 minutes of the time Libby did some writing on her paper and the rest of the time she looked out of the window.

Draw a pie chart to show how Libby spent the hour.

Remember the whole circle represents one hour.

**5**

Six of the children at Subset House have been learning to measure distances on a map. Using a good map they each worked out how far one town was from Manchester. Mr Delta, the Geography teacher, asked them to draw a bar chart showing these distances.

Here are the children's discoveries.

*Distances from Manchester*

Tom
   SHEFFIELD 38 miles

Hamish
   BOLTON 11 miles

Emma
   BRADFORD 34 miles

Libby
   PRESTON 30 miles

Jonathan
   BURNLEY 24 miles

Jean-Pierre
   CHESTER 38 miles

Use (a) to (f) below to help you to draw a bar chart to show how far each town is from Manchester.

**a)** Put the children's discoveries in order of distance starting with the nearest to Manchester.

**b)** Let one small square represent 2 miles.

**c)** Put the miles across the page.

**d)** Put the towns up the page.

**e)** Draw a neat bar chart.

**f)** Remember to put a title.

# 7. Number ii

> A *factor* is a number which will divide exactly into another number.
> For example, 5 is a factor of 15, so $15 \div 5 = 3$.

**1**

*Speedily* work out two pairs of factors for each of the following. For example, 32: 4, 8 and 2, 16.

a) 36    b) 16    c) 40    d) 24    e) 100

f) 56    g) 28    h) 30    i) 60    j) 25

**\*2**

Copy and fill in this number square. Note that the sign tells you to ADD. Try to find quick ways and time yourself for filling in the whole square.

| + | 5 | 9 | 8 | 12 | 7 |
|---|---|---|---|----|---|
| 6 | 11 | | | | |
| 16 | | 25 | | | |
| 26 | | | | | |
| 36 | | | | | |
| 46 | | | | | |

59

**3**

Add the following lists of numbers and then find the odd answer out.

a) $26 + 5 + 19 + 16 + 8$

b) $29 + 15 + 18 + 6 + 6$

c) $19 + 19 + 5 + 5 + 26$

d) $7 + 7 + 7 + 7 + 7 + 7 + 7 + 7 + 7$

**4**

Look at the numbers below and try to write 3 more for each list.
Tom has done one for you:

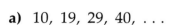

3, 6, 10, 15, . . .     21    28    36

> *3 (+3) makes 6*
> *6 (+4) makes 10*
> *10 (+5) makes 15*
> *so the next 3 numbers must be*
> *15 (+6) makes 21*
> *21 (+7) makes 28*
> *28 (+8) makes 36*

a) 10, 19, 29, 40, . . .

b) 5, 10, 16, 23, . . .

c) 30, 35, 41, 48, . . .

d) 250, 240, 220, 190, . . .

**5**

In 'Number ii' Jonathan, Libby and Hamish played a card game in which they had to collect sets of cards.

Hamish collected the following sets. Explain in words what sets he had been collecting.

For example, 10, 25, 35, 5 (all divide by 5).

**a)** 6, 22, 14, 4, 8

**b)** 7, 49, 28, 56, 84

**c)** 11, 13, 7, 15, 9

**d)** 33, 132, 110, 66, 121

**e)** 81, 72, 63, 54

# PRACTICE 2 (B)

 **1**

*Speedily* add the following looking for quick ways of doing the calculation.

| | | | |
|---|---|---|---|
| **a)** 27 + 9 | **b)** 37 + 9 | **c)** 19 + 57 | **d)** 67 + 29 |
| **e)** 89 + 17 | **f)** 18 + 13 | **g)** 28 + 23 | **h)** 73 + 28 |
| **i)** 68 + 43 | **j)** 58 + 33 | | |

To round off a number to the nearest hundred: when the last 2 figures are 49 or less round down to the lower hundred, for example 349 becomes 300. When the last 2 figures are 50 or more round up to the upper hundred, for example 352 becomes 400.

**2**

*Speedily* round these numbers to the nearest hundred.

a) 444     b) 597     c) 836     d) 758     e) 319

f) 987     g) 748     h) 750     i) 333     j) 619

**3**

Write down the following numbers in figures and beside them write each number to the nearest thousand. (Use column headings to help if you need to.)

For example, thirty thousand and four would be 30004 which is 30000 to the nearest thousand.

**a)** nine hundred and fifteen

**b)** seventy thousand four hundred and forty

**c)** nineteen thousand five hundred

**d)** one thousand one hundred

**e)** five hundred and thirteen

**f)** ten thousand four hundred and ninety-nine

**4**

Using one of the quick methods you have learnt, work out the answers to these questions in your head.

How much change would you have from £1 after spending:

a) 89p

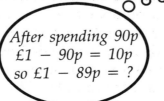

After spending 90p
£1 − 90p = 10p
so £1 − 89p = ?

**b)** 31p + 68p

**c)** 61p + 10p

**d)** 22p + 37p

**e)** 3p + 19p + 50p?

How much change from £5 would you have after spending:

**f)** £3.50 + £1.19

**g)** £4.92 + 8p

**h)** £1.21 + £2.01

**i)** £2.99 + £1.99

**j)** £2.50 + £0.71?

# SUMMARY

 **1**

*Speedily* work out these:

**a)** 6 × 5 × 2

**b)** 2 × 6 × 5

**c)** 5 × 2 × 6

**d)** 6 × 2 × 5

**e)** 5 × 6 × 2

**f)** 2 × 5 × 6

 **2**

All your answers to question 1 should have been the same. Now multiply these and then write a sentence saying what you notice about your answers.

**a)** 2 × 5 × 2

**b)** 4 × 5 × 2

**c)** 10 × 8 × 1

**d)** 8 × 5 × 4

**e)** 4 × 4 × 5 × 2 × 2

**3**

If you were playing a game and moved from 6 to 14 work out what number pairs you might have thrown using two dice.

For example, *from 6 to 14* (you move 8 squares):

a 6 and a 2
a 4 and a 4
a 5 and a 3

Work out 2 pairs for each of the following moves:

**a)** from 19 to 24

**b)** from 63 to 71

**c)** from 83 to 90

**d)** from 33 to 39

**e)** from 54 to 64

**f)** from 21 to 24

 When the last 3 figures are 499 or less round down to the lower thousand, for example 1498 becomes 1000. When the last 3 figures are 500 or more, round up to the upper thousand, for example 1500 becomes 2000.

 **4**

Round these numbers to the nearest 1000.

| | | | |
|---|---|---|---|
| **a)** 1057 | **b)** 2330 | **c)** 6937 | **d)** 1200 |
| **e)** 4499 | **f)** 5500 | **g)** 3864 | **h)** 1328 |
| **i)** 1001 | **j)** 9999 | | |

**5**

Try to find a quick way to work out the following:

**a)** 56 + 99

**b)** 580 ÷ 10

**c)** 100 − 55

**d)** 65 − 19

**e)** 18 × 10

**f)** 29p + 15p

**g)** 146 − 47

**h)** £5.40 ÷ 10

**i)** 169 mm + 31 mm

 **6**

Here is a table showing toll prices for crossing a new bridge. By writing the number of vehicles crossing to the nearest 10 or 100 or 1000, work out approximately how much money is collected in tolls each day.

| Vehicle | Number crossing | Charge |
|---------|-----------------|--------|
| Buses | 59 | £1 |
| Cars | 3508 | 20 p |
| Lorries/Vans | 749 | 50 p |

 ***7**

Libby's Number Line Game.

*In my game you need two dice of different colours or sizes, a counter for each player and a number line. We will call the dice A and B.*

A          B

Decide which die will be A and which will be B.

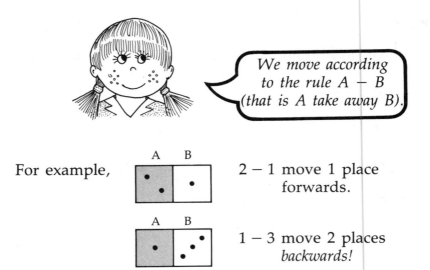

We move according to the rule A − B (that is A take away B).

For example,

A    B

2 − 1 move 1 place forwards.

A    B

1 − 3 move 2 places *backwards!*

Play Libby's game on a number line. You need at least 2 players. The winner could be the first player to land on top of another when his/her turn comes. If you prefer, make up a game of your own, using 2 dice.

# ALLSORTS

 **\*1**

Copy these squares and fill in the missing numbers. Take each sign as it comes. The top line has been done for you.

| 2 | × | 5 | − | 3 | = 7 |
|---|---|---|---|---|---|
| + |  | × |  | × |  |
|  | + | 3 | − |  | = 1 |
| − |  | − |  | ÷ |  |
|  | × | 6 | ÷ | 8 | = 6 |
| = 0 |  |  |  | = 3 |  |

| 7 | × | 2 | − | 5 | = 9 |
|---|---|---|---|---|---|
| × |  | + |  | + |  |
|  | × | 6 | + |  | = 9 |
| + |  | ÷ |  | − |  |
| 1 | + |  | − | 5 |  |
| = 1 |  | = 1 |  | = 9 |  |

66

**2**

Each shape stands for a number in a secret code. The value of the shape is the same each time it appears. Work out what each shape must be worth.

**a)** ▲ × ● = 8

● + ● + ● + ● = 8

What is ● worth?
What is ▲ worth?

**b)** ■ × ■ = ■ + ■ + ■ + ■ + ■
■ + ■ + ■ + ■ + ■

What is ■ worth?

**c)** $\dfrac{\int}{●} = 3$

What is ∫ worth?

 **3**

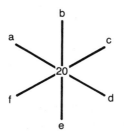

Place one of the numbers 18, 22, 12, 26, 14, 28 in place of each letter (a, b, c, etc.), so that when they are added to the 20 in the middle, the answer for each line is 60.

 **\*4**

**a)** Copy the multiplication square on the next page.

**b)** With a stopwatch or ordinary digital watch, time yourself as you fill it in. As soon as you have finished, write down your time.

**c)** Check each answer carefully. If you have made a mistake, or if your time is more than 6 minutes, then you do not know your tables well enough!

A time of under 2 minutes 30 seconds, with no mistakes, is very good indeed.

67

# TEAM TASK

Perhaps your teacher would allow you to organise a table square competition? A weekly competition is quite exciting. (Notice the table square below goes up to 11.)

| × | 3 | 7 | 6 | 10 | 4 | 8 | 5 | 9 | 11 | 2 |
|----|---|---|---|----|---|---|---|---|----|---|
| 10 | | | | | | | | | | |
| 5 | | | | | | | | | | |
| 11 | | | | | | | | | | |
| 6 | | | | | | | | | | |
| 9 | | | | | | | | | | |
| 3 | | | | | | | | | | |
| 8 | | | | | | | | | | |
| 7 | | | | | | | | | | |
| 4 | | | | | | | | | | |
| 2 | | | | | | | | | | |

 **5**

Mrs Haddock is working out approximately how much money she needs to pay the butcher for this week's order. She has £80 left to spend this week. The list below tells you how much the butcher will charge. Approximate the cost of each item and see if she has enough to pay for them all.

10 chickens at £2.99 each.

5 kg sausages at £2.49 each kg.

60 pork chops at 59p each chop.

(*Hint*: Work out 10 chops at 60p each then times your answer by ? .)

# 8. Angles ii

## PRACTICE 1 (AB)

 **1**

Estimate the size of the following angles to the nearest 10°:

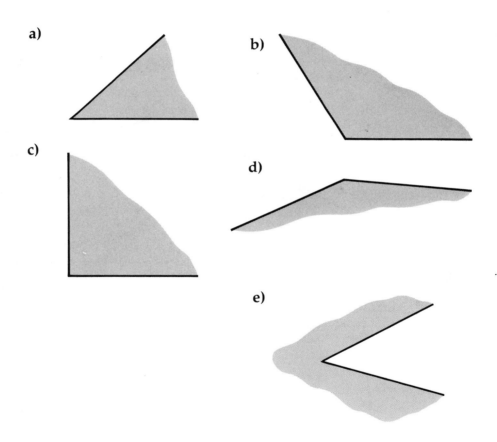

**a)**

**b)**

**c)**

**d)**

**e)**

 **2**

Write the following angles to the nearest 5°, saying what kind of angle each is:

**a)** 122°

**b)** 43°

**c)** 222°

**d)** 84°

**e)** 176°

69

## 3

Measure the following angles to the nearest 5°, and write down what kind of angle each is:

**a)**

**b)**

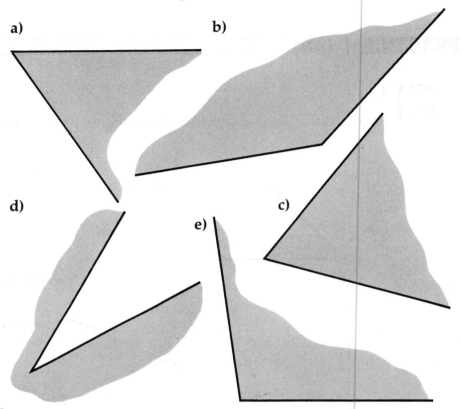

**d)**

**c)**

**e)**

## 4

Measure the angles *a* to *f* in the diagram to the nearest 5°.

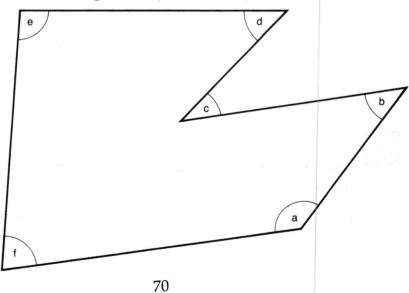

**5**

Draw a base line AB for *each* of the following angles. Draw the first 3 angles from A and the last 2 from B.
For example:

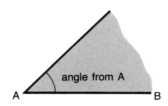 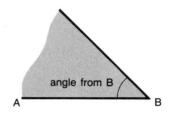

**a)** 35°          **b)** 120°          **c)** 155°

**d)** 85°          **e)** 105°

# PRACTICE 2 (C)

**1**

Libby is standing in the centre of the playing field at Subset House. She is facing the buildings, which are due North.

**a)** Mark a point L to represent Libby and draw a North–South line through L.

 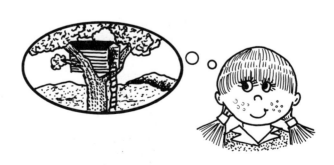

**b)** The angle measurement (bearing) of her tree-hut from where she is standing is 55°. Draw a line and mark a point T to show where her tree-hut could be.

71

**2**

Look at the diagram below. Write down the angle measurements of Tom (T), Jean-Pierre (J-P) and Hamish (H) from Jonathan (J).

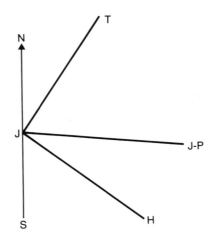

**3**

**a)** Jean-Pierre is now standing where Jonathan was in the diagram for question 2. Draw a new diagram and place Jonathan so that his bearing is 180° from Jean-Pierre.

**b)** Place Libby on a bearing of 360° from Jean-Pierre.

**c)** Hamish is still in the same position. Show Fatima on a bearing of 90° east of Hamish.

**d)** Tom now moves. On the same diagram mark Tom on a bearing of 270° from Hamish.

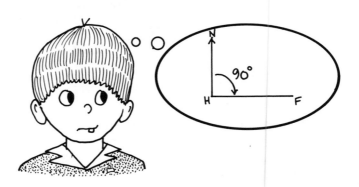

# SUMMARY

**1**

Estimate the size of the following angles to the nearest 10°.
Say what kind of angle each is.

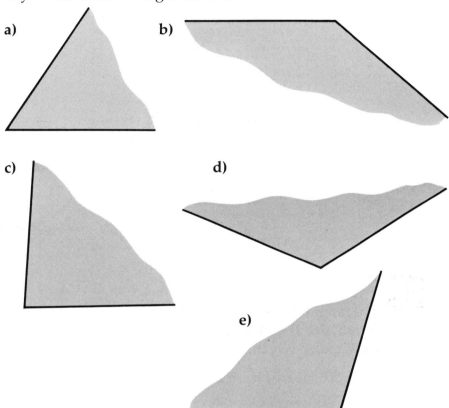

a)

b)

c)

d)

e)

**2**

Measure the angles in question 1 above, giving your
answer to the nearest 5°.

**3**

Write the following angles correct to the nearest 5°, and
then make neat, accurate drawings of your answers:

a)  134°          b)  68°          c)  106°

d)  221°          e)  84°

**4**

The diagram below shows Mrs Haddock standing in the middle of the kitchen at Subset House. Use your triangular protractor to give the bearing of the various objects from Mrs Haddock.

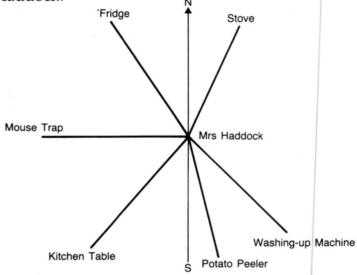

 **5**

The angle measurements (bearings) of 5 of Emma's friends, when she is standing in the middle of the classroom and facing due North, are:

Tom 30°, Jean-Pierre 85°, Hamish 120°, Libby 225°, Jonathan 350°.

Make a neat drawing to show this information.

# ALLSORTS

 **1**

Look at the diagram which shows the four points of the compass.

If you stand facing North and turn clockwise through $\frac{1}{2}$ a revolution, you are then facing South.

**a)** If you stand facing East and turn clockwise through $\frac{3}{4}$ of a revolution, in which direction are you now facing?

**b)** How many degrees is this?

**c)** What kind of angle have you turned through?

**2**

Draw your own diagram showing the four points of the compass, like the one below. You will notice that in this diagram, an extra line exactly halfway between North and East has been added; this direction is North East (NE).

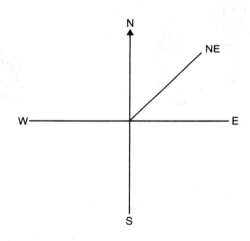

**a)** Draw in lines to show: South East (SE); South West (SW); North West (NW).

**b)** How many degrees are there between E and SE?

**c)** What kind of angle is it?

**d)** How many degrees are there between NE and W if I turn clockwise?

**e)** What kind of angle is this?

**f)** If I face NW and turn clockwise through $1\frac{1}{2}$ revolutions, in which direction will I be facing?

**\*3**

Hamish's father has an old fashioned wrist-watch, one with an hour hand, a minute hand and a second hand.

a) Find out the proper name for a watch of this kind. (It is NOT a digital watch!)

b) The second hand goes once round the watch every minute. How many degrees is this, and what special name do we give to the angle it has turned?

c) Through how many degrees does the minute hand turn in half an hour? What special name do we give to this sort of angle?

d) Work out how many degrees the hour hand turns through in one hour. What sort of angle is this?

e) Find out some ways people used to tell the time before clocks and watches were invented.

f) Try and make a model of a piece of apparatus to tell the time.

**4**

Measure the angles in the diagram to the nearest 5°. Make the measurements in alphabetical order.

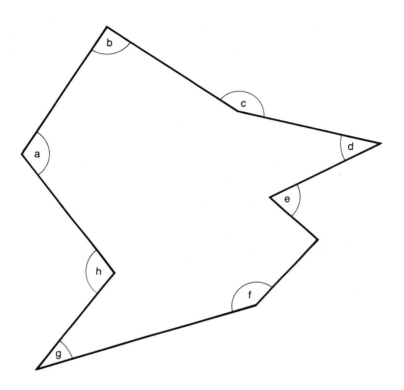

**5**

The diagrams below show some wheels with equally spaced spokes.

(1)                                    (2)

77

(3)                                  (4)

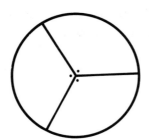 

Now answer these questions:

**a)** What fraction of a revolution is the angle between two
spokes in each diagram?
For example, in (2) each angle is $\frac{1}{4}$ of a revolution.

**b)** What size is the angle between the spokes in each
diagram? (*Hint*: A revolution is 360°.)

# 9. Measurement ii

## PRACTICE 1 (A)

$$1 \text{ m } = 100 \text{ cm}$$
$$1 \text{ cm } = 10 \text{ mm}$$

 **1**

*Speedily* write these lengths in cm, using decimals if necessary.

a) 50 mm          b) 55 mm          c) 600 mm

d) 23 mm          e) 37 cm 6 mm     f) 6 cm 9 mm

g) 160 mm         h) 66 cm 6 mm

Perimeter is the distance all the way round the edge of a shape.

 **2**

Find the perimeters of these figures, putting your results in a table. The side of each *small* square is 1 cm.

| Shape | Perimeter (in cm) |
|---|---|
| a) | |
| b) | |
| c) | |
| d) | |
| e) | |

a)

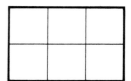

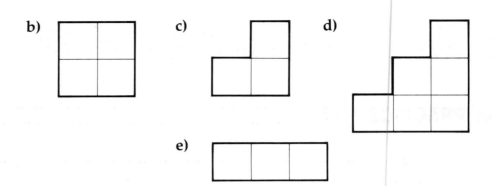

**b)**  **c)**  **d)**

**e)**

 **3**

This diagram shows a lawn with a rose bed in the middle.
The rose bed is 20 m by 10 m.

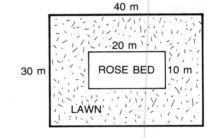

**a)** What is the perimeter of the rose bed?

**b)** What is the perimeter of the outside of the lawn?

**c)** What is the total perimeter of the rose bed and the outside of the lawn?

 **4**

Find the perimeters of the following shapes. Use cm and mm and record your results in a table, like the one below. (Shape 1) has been started for you.)

| Sides | Shape 1 | Shape 2 | Shape 3 | Shape 4 |
|---|---|---|---|---|
| a = | 3 cm | | | |
| b = | | | | |
| c = | | | | |
| d = | | | | |
| e = | 2 cm 3 mm | | | |
| Total = | | | | |

**Shape 1**

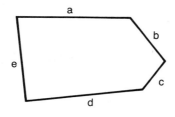

**Shape 2**

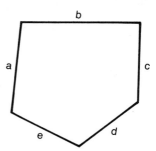

**Shape 3**

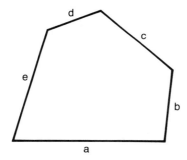

**Shape 4**

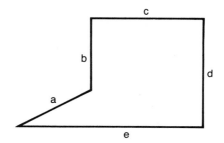

# PRACTICE 2 (BC)

 **1**

*Speedily* find the areas of the shapes (a) to (e) of Practice 1, question 2, by counting the squares of each shape.

Area can be worked out by counting squares, and often found by counting just the number of rows and the number of squares in each row.

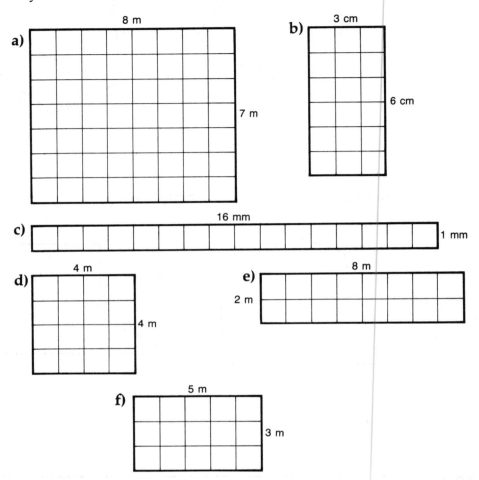

**2**

Find the areas of these rectangles, remembering to give your answers in the correct units.

a) 8 m / 7 m

b) 3 cm / 6 cm

c) 16 mm / 1 mm

d) 4 m / 4 m

e) 8 m / 2 m

f) 5 m / 3 m

**3**

Look at the diagram below from question 3 of Practice 1.

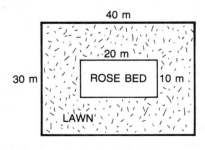

a) What is the area of the rose bed itself?

b) What is the area of the lawn and the rose bed together?

c) What is the area of the lawn?

**\*4**

**a)** *Estimate* the number of square centimetres in the
following shapes:

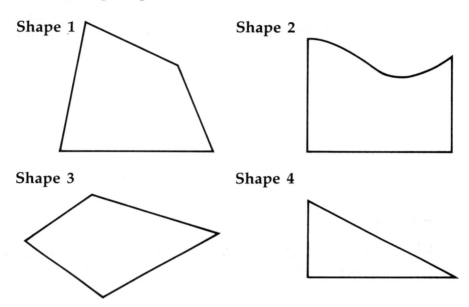

**Shape 1**        **Shape 2**

**Shape 3**        **Shape 4**

**b)** Now trace the shapes onto cm squared paper and, by
counting the squares, work out the approximate area of
each shape.

If more than half of any square is inside the shape,
count this as a whole square; if less than half, do not
count it. Use the example below to help you. The
squares with dots in are counted as whole squares.

*Remember* these are cm squares.

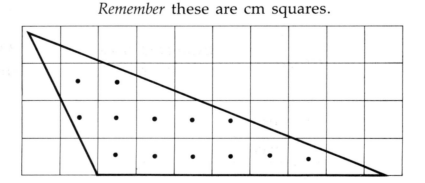

There are 12 squares with dots in, so the area is about
12 cm².

**c)** Now record your answers for (a) and (b) in a table, like the one below.

| Shape | Estimated area in cm² | Area by counting squares (cm²) |
|---|---|---|
| 1 | | |
| 2 | | |
| 3 | | |
| 4 | | |

 **\*5**

You will need a simple balance and a set of standard masses. Work with a partner, if your teacher will allow you to.

**a)** Estimate the masses of the following objects (write your answers in grams):

PSM Ø Workbook, a tennis ball, 3 pens, a large dictionary

**b)** Now use the balance and the set of masses to find the masses of the objects in (a). Set your answers out in a table like the one below:

| Object | Estimated mass (in g) | Mass (in g) |
|---|---|---|
| PSM Ø Workbook | | |
| Tennis ball | | |
| 3 pens | | |
| Large dictionary | | |

# SUMMARY

**1**

*Speedily* find the perimeters of these shapes. All measurements are given in cm.

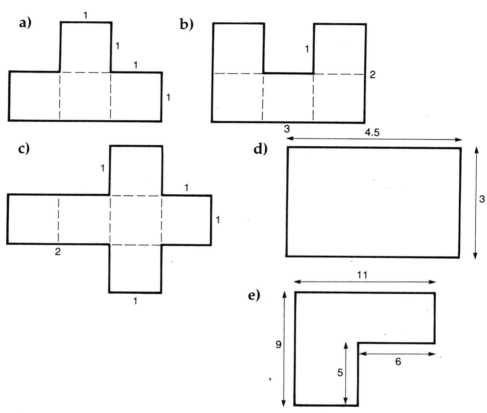

**2**

*Speedily* find the areas of the shapes in question 1.

**\*3**

This shape has a perimeter of 12 cm and an area of 6 cm².

**a)** Draw another shape which has an area of 12 cm².

**b)** Draw *two* different shapes which both have a perimeter of 16 cm.

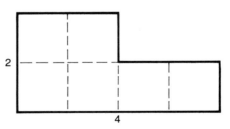

85

**\*4**

Trace this shape carefully
then cut along the lines.

Rearrange the pieces to
make a square.

Area does not change
when it is cut up.

What is the area of the
shape?

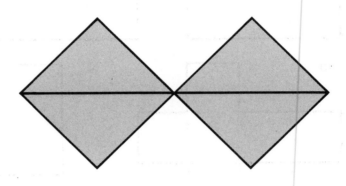

**5**

Work out the areas of these shapes. The first one has been
done for you. All the measurements are given in cm.

**a)**

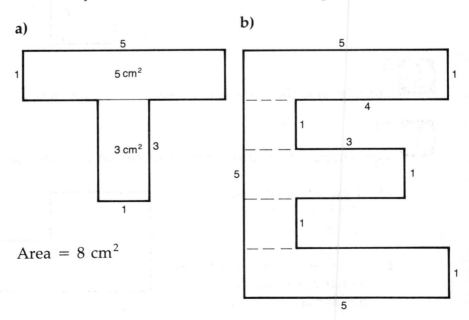

Area = 8 cm²

**b)**

86

**c)**

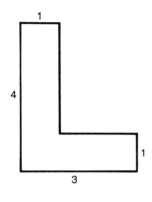

**d)**

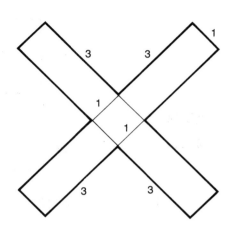

 **\*6**

**a)** Using a simple balance like the one in 'Measurement ii' Book B, find the mass of your mathematics exercise book.

**b)** What is the total mass of the mathematics exercise books of all the children in your form? Write your answer in kg.

# ALLSORTS ══════════════════════════════

 **1**

**a)** Draw this figure for yourself carefully (this diagram is NOT accurate).

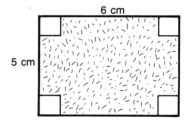

You may use the squares in your exercise book to help.

Find the dotted area.

All 4 little squares are 1 cm by 1 cm.

**b)** Do the same with this figure:

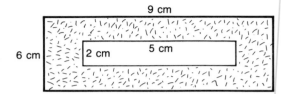

9 cm

6 cm

2 cm

5 cm

**\*2**

**a)** Runners doing the 1500 m race run quite a long way. How far is this distance in km?

**b)** Try to see how long it takes you to walk 1500 m.

**\*3**

Use a sports reference book to find out who is the present 1500 m world champion. What is the world record for the 1500 m?

**\*4**

**a)** You will need a 5 ml plastic spoon and a tablespoon. (Note: a medicine spoon is 5 ml.)
How many 5 ml spoons filled with water have the same capacity as a tablespoon?

**b)** You will need a 5 ml plastic spoon and an ordinary tea cup.

How many 5 ml spoons will it take to fill an ordinary teacup?

**c)** Use your answer to (b) to work out roughly how many teacups make 1 litre.

**d)** Get a litre container (a plastic 1 litre lemonade bottle will do). Check your answer to (c) by pouring the correct number of cupfuls into the container.

**\*5**

Try to walk round a square kilometre. Time how long it takes you.

# 10. Sets

 **1**

*Speedily* write down which group or set the following lists belong to:

a) rose, daffodil, crocus, snowdrop, tulip

b) 6, 10, 2, 8, 14, 16, 20

c) Jim, James, John, Jonathan, Julian

d) Cathy, Ann, Susan, Emma, Mary

e) orange, plum, grape, apple, pear

f) arm, toe, hand, face, nose

g) N, P, A, D, F, Z

h) chair, table, cupboard, shelf, drawer

i) tea, coffee, cocoa, Ovaltine, chocolate

j) tennis, rugby, hockey, cricket, football

 **2**

Here is a collection of things found in Jonathan's case:

An orange, a rubber band, a small ball of string, an empty match-box, a pen, a pencil, one of his dad's golf balls, a ruler, part of Tuesday's packed lunch, and a pencil sharpener.

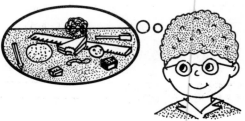

**a)** Write down one group of things that have something in common.

**b)** Write down another group.

**c)** Can you find a third group (think about the shape of the things, where you might find them and what they are used for)?

 **3**

Draw diagrams for the three groups from question 1, remembering to mark each diagram with a letter for that group.

 **4**

Here are some groups. Write down the name of each group, followed by five things you could put in it.

**a)** Teachers at my school.

**b)** My friends.

**c)** Food I like.

**d)** Toys in my bedroom.

 **5**

Draw diagrams for your groups in question 4.

# PRACTICE 2 (B)

 **1**

*Speedily* write down one more element which will fit in to the following sets; you do *not* need to copy the complete list.

**a)** {brother, mother, cousin, father, ............................. }

**b)** {up, down, near, behind, ...................................... }

**c)** {hairbrush, broom, paintbrush, ............................. }

**d)** {cat, budgie, goldfish, hamster, ............................. }

**e)** {boot, soot, hoot, root, ........................................ }

**f)** {history, mathematics, geography, art, ..................... }

**g)** {060, 050, 030, 080, 010, ....................................... }

**h)** {circle, triangle, rectangle, ................................... }

**i)** {screwdriver, nails, hammer, ................................. }

**j)** {butcher, fishmonger, greengrocer, ......................... }

 **2**

Write out the following elements using SET LANGUAGE. For example, cat, dog, hamster, gerbil ∈ {pets}.

**a)** cow, sheep, pig, chicken.

**b)** pound, franc, lira, peseta.

**c)** England, Scotland, Wales, Northern Ireland.

**d)** M1, M2, M3, M4, M5, M6, M8, M25, M62.

**e)** boat, ship, tanker, tug, ferry, speed boat.

**3**

Write the following sentences in mathematical language.

**a)** Rose is a member of the set, garden flowers.

**b)** Toothbrush is a member of the set, things found in the bathroom.

**c)** Mathematics is a member of the set, school subjects.

**d)** Alps is a member of the set, mountain ranges.

**e)** Shirt is a member of the set, clothes.

 **4**

Write the following mathematical sentences in proper English:

**a)** carpet $\in$ {floor coverings}

**b)** Isle of Wight $\in$ {islands off the English coast}

**c)** France $\in$ {countries of Europe}

**d)** Atlantic $\in$ {oceans of the world}

**e)** Mickey Mouse $\in$ {cartoon characters}

**5**

Find the odd one out in the following sets; write your answers in set language.

For example, {table, chair, bed, mouse, dressing-table}
*Answer*: mouse ∉ {furniture}

a) {car, bus, plane, coach, taxi}

b) {pineapple, banana, pea, orange, peach}

c) {Manchester, London, Brighton, New York, Durham}

d) {centimetre, metre, gram, kilometre, decimetre}

e) {2, 3, 4, 8, 10, 12, 14}

**6**

Draw Venn diagrams of the following sets. Write the elements in the diagram and remember to draw freehand loops. Set out your answers like the example.

For example, Manchester, Birmingham, Nottingham, Liverpool, Norwich
*Answer*: C = {cities of England}

a) Devon, Sussex, Surrey, Yorkshire, Lancashire

b) France, Italy, Spain, Portugal, Austria

c) 1, 3, 5, 7, 9

d) a, r, q, s, t, z

e) chicken, turkey, beef, lamb, pork

# SUMMARY

 **1**

*Speedily* write true or false for each of the following:

a) table ∈ {things you sit on}

b) rubber ∉ {things to write with}

c) motor-racing ∉ {dangerous sports}

d) lemonade ∈ {drinks}

e) BBC Microcomputer ∉ {computers}

f) girl ∉ {people}

g) 60 ∈ {numbers which divide exactly by 20}

h) 121 ∈ {numbers which read the same back to front}

i) Libby ∉ {PSM children}

j) August ∈ {days of the week}

Did someone mention my name?

 **2**

a) Make a list of the children in your class.

b) Sort the children into five different sets—again using set language when you list the sets in your book.

94

**3**

Write down the elements of the following sets using set language:

a) The multiples of 3 up to 40.

b) The multiples of 4 up to 50.

c) The multiples of 7 up to 90.

d) The multiples of 9 up to 110.

 **\*4**

Make a collection of about twenty different things which will fit on top of your desk.

a) Write down a list of these things.

b) Sort them out into as many different sets as you can. Make sure you list these sets carefully in your book using correct set language. When you have listed ten sets show your teacher.

c) Make Venn diagrams for three of the sets, writing the elements on the diagrams.

# ALLSORTS

 **1**

a) See how many different sets you can make from the following elements:

headlights, vase, record, ruler, spoon, fork, pen, plate, steering wheel, scissors, paper, cup, diary, spare wheel, plug, shelf, picture, television, computer, knife, indicator.

**b)** Find out who has made the most sets when the rest of your class have done (a). Then make a list for the wall.

 **2**

Look at the following sets; eight elements belong to more than one set. Pick out the ones which do and write your answer like the example.

For example, A = {hamster, gerbil, bat, rabbit};
B = {pads, stumps, bat, bails}
*Answer*: bat ∈ A and bat ∈ B

P  = {2, 4, 6, 8, 10, 12, 14, 16}

Q  = {dog, hamster, cat, gerbil}

R  = {hammer, nails, saw, chisel}

S  = {mouse, cat, spider, fly}

T  = {6, 12, 18, 24, 30, 36, 42}

V  = {sawdust, saw, bench, chisel}

W = {lion, tiger, cat, leopard}

X  = {3, 6, 9, 12, 15}

Y  = {plane, bird, fly, helicopter}

Z  = {2, 3, 5, 7, 11, 13, 17}

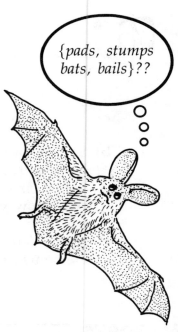

96

# 11. Number iii

## PRACTICE 1 (AB)

 **1**

*Speedily* fill in the missing signs:

a)  6    8 = 48          b)  6    8 = 14

c)  6    8 = $\frac{3}{4}$          d)  20    10 = 2

e)  (6  6)  6 = 6          f)  1    1 = 1

g)  1    1 = 0          h)  1    1 = 1

i)  1  1  1 = 1          j)  12    0 = 0

 **2**

Draw pictures to show the following:

a)  3 × 6 eggs

b)  (3 + 6) eggs

c)  (6 − 3) eggs

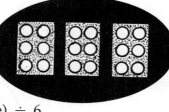

d)  (30 flowers) ÷ 6

e)  (3 bars of chocolate) ÷ 6

To divide 441 by 21 you can use factors.
21 = 7 × 3, so
441 ÷ 7 = 63 and then
63 ÷ 3 = 21.
So 441 ÷ 21 = 21.

 **3**

Fatima wants to share 144 marbles among 18 people. She is going to play a team game and needs to make sure all 3 teams have the same number of marbles for each of the six people in the team.

**a)** How many marbles will there be for each team?

**b)** How many marbles will there be for each person in each team?

**c)** How many 18s are there in 144?

 **4**

In question 3 Fatima divided first by 3 and then by 6. Use 2 other factors of 18 to work out 324 ÷ 18.

 **5**

Write these numbers as a number (factor) times itself.

For example, 100 = 10 × 10

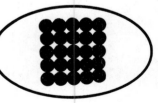

**a)** 25 =    ×

**b)** 49 =    ×

**c)** 144 =    ×

**d)** 81 =    ×

e)    1 =    ×

f)    4 =    ×

g)  121 =    ×

h)   36 =    ×

i)   16 =    ×

j)    9 =    ×

# PRACTICE 2 (CD)

*Speedily* write down the sign which goes with these words:

**1**

a) difference

b) product

c) total

d) minus

e) sum

f) division

g) plus

h) multiply

i) times

j) subtract

To check if a number divides exactly by 3, add the digits and if the total divides by 3, so does the number.

**2**

**a)** Which of these numbers can be divided exactly by 3:

630, 214, 161, 342, 1002?

**b)** List the numbers which can be divided exactly by 5:

1005, 38, 415, 900, 175

**3**

Miss Layshun is trying to work out how much the tickets will cost for a school outing to a computer exhibition.

50 children and 4 adults will go and they will pay 95p for each adult and 60p for each child.

**a)** Work out the cost of the adults' tickets.

**b)** Work out the cost of the children's tickets.

**c)** Work out the cost of all 54 tickets.

**4**

How much does the school secretary spend in the post office if she buys

36 stamps at 17p each and

24 stamps at 14p each?

**5**

Jonathan has smudged his long multiplication in his exercise book. Try to fill in the missing numbers.

# SUMMARY

 **1**

*Speedily* complete the following:

a) To multiply by 17, multiply by 7 and then by .............. and add together both answers.

b) To multiply by 23, first multiply by 3 and then by ........ and add together both answers.

c) To multiply by 16, first multiply by 6 and then by ........ and add together both answers.

d) If you multiply by 5, then by 50 and add together both answers, you are multiplying by ...............................

e) If you multiply by 3, then by 30 and add together both answers, you are multiplying by ...............................

 **2**

a) The sum of two numbers is 300. If one is 163, what is the other?

**b)** How much less than 2 kg is 1 kg 325 g?

**c)** What is the total of 25 km + 87 km + 69 km?

**d)** The product of 2 numbers is 400. One of the numbers is 20. What is the other?

**e)** The total shopping bill came to £6.85. If Mrs Haddock bought bread costing £1.85 and eggs costing £4.20, how much did the sugar cost?

 **3**

A large order of eggs has arrived at school. There are 312 eggs. They come in trays holding 2 dozen eggs in each tray. How many trays of eggs are there? *Hint:* Remember you can divide by large numbers using factors.

 **4**

Tom was fed up waiting for his mum in the supermarket so he began to count the tins of soup on the shelves. There were 15 rows of 26 tins of soup.

How many tins were there altogether?

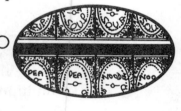

 **5**

Libby has a problem. She is working out what she needs for the school sale but she has muddled up her calculations. See if you can help Libby to find out which kind of calculation goes with each problem.

**a)** Libby needs enough baking trays to make 166 cakes. (The trays make 12 cakes at a time.)

**b)** Libby needs enough sweets for each child in the school to have 1 sweet each. There are 14 classes and 22 children in each class.

**c)** Libby has 308 balloons and wants to know if there are enough balloons for each pupil in each class.

Choose and write down the correct calculations to work out each of Libby's problems. (There are 2 more than you need.) Draw diagrams to help you if you like.

14 × 22,          166 + 12,          ?

308 ÷ 14,          22 × 14.

166 ÷ 12

# ALLSORTS

**1**

Below are some large numbers. Check if they divide exactly by 2, 3 and 5. (If you have forgotten how to check this, look in Book B, 'Number iii', Section D.)

Copy the table and fill in the spaces. The first line is done for you.

|      | ÷ 2 | ÷ 3 | ÷ 5 |
|------|-----|-----|-----|
| 6939 | ✗   | ✓   | ✗   |
| 3402 |     |     |     |
| 5000 |     |     |     |
| 8999 |     |     |     |
| 7893 |     |     |     |

**2**

Jonathan has begun collecting stamps. Work out how many stamps he has in his album from the following countries:

**a)** France: 6 pages with 8 rows of stamps and 5 stamps on each row.

**b)** Germany: 2 pages, 7 rows on each with 6 stamps on each row.

103

**c)** Holland: 1 page of 9 rows and 7 stamps on each row.

**d)** Great Britain: 10 pages with 15 stamps on each page.

**e)** How many stamps has Jonathan altogether?

**f)** From which of the 4 countries does he have most stamps?

 **\*3**

Copy this crossnumber and answer the clues.

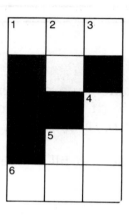

ACROSS
1. 15 × 15
5. $\frac{1}{2}$ of 104
6. Another way of saying $\frac{1}{4}$ past 5

DOWN
2. 13 plus 13
3. (10 − 6) + 1
4. 25 × 33
5. Product of 3 and 17

# 12. Fractions ii

## PRACTICE 1 (AB)

 **1**

*Speedily* copy and complete the flow chart to show how to change $3\frac{3}{4}$ into an improper fraction.

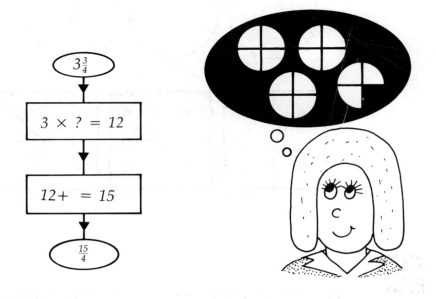

$3\frac{3}{4}$

$3 \times ? = 12$

$12+ = 15$

$\frac{15}{4}$

 **2**

In each of these examples, write the mixed number and then change it to an improper fraction.

For example:

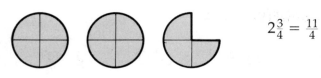

$2\frac{3}{4} = \frac{11}{4}$

105

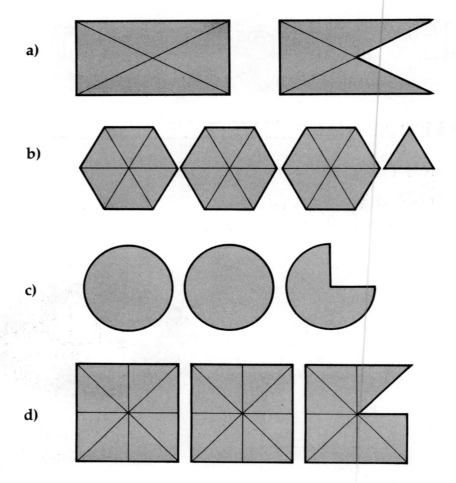

**a)**

**b)**

**c)**

**d)**

 **3**

Change these mixed numbers to improper fractions:

a) $1\frac{3}{4}$     b) $3\frac{1}{3}$     c) $5\frac{6}{7}$     d) $10\frac{9}{10}$     e) $50\frac{1}{3}$

 **4**

Change these improper fractions to whole numbers.

For example, $\frac{4}{2} = 2$.

a) $\frac{21}{3}$     b) $\frac{25}{5}$     c) $\frac{70}{7}$     d) $\frac{63}{9}$     e) $\frac{48}{6}$

**5**

Mrs Haddock has been cutting up some cake for tea on Sports Day. She wants at least 4 whole cakes on each table. Each cake has been cut up into small pieces, sometimes into 5 pieces or 9 pieces, 8 pieces or even 10 pieces.

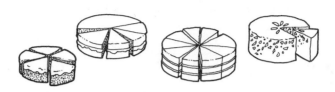

Look at the list below and write down which tables have at *least* 4 whole cakes on them.

| Table 1 | Table 2 | Table 3 | Table 4 | Table 5 |
|---------|---------|---------|---------|---------|
| $\frac{32}{8}$ | $\frac{18}{5}$ | $\frac{42}{10}$ | $\frac{36}{5}$ | $\frac{38}{9}$ |

# PRACTICE 2 (CD)

**1**

*Speedily* write the amounts below as hundredths of £1 and as a decimal fraction of £1.

For example, $8\text{ p} = £\frac{8}{100} = £0.08$

a) 81p

b) 19p

c) 55p

d) 1p

e) 76p

*I think I'll stick to cutting up cakes!*

**2**

Write the following centimetre measurements as whole metres and decimal fractions of 1 m.

For example, 125 cm = 1.25 m

**a)** 36 cm        **b)** 285 cm        **c)** 9 cm

**d)** 451 cm        **e)** 799 cm

 **\*3**

Here is a picture of $1\frac{4}{5}$:

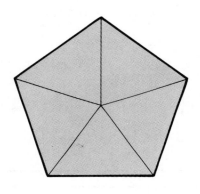 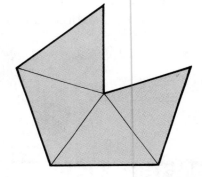

**a)** Trace the shapes above.

**b)** On your tracing, divide each fifth into 2 equal pieces.

**c)** What fraction of each whole shape is each small piece?

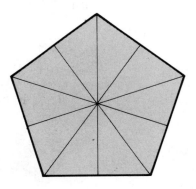

**d)** Write $\frac{1}{10}$ as a decimal fraction.

**e)** Write $\frac{4}{5}$ as a decimal fraction. (Remember decimal fractions are to do with tenths, hundredths, etc.)

**f)** Write $1\frac{4}{5}$ as a decimal fraction.

 **4**

Look at these numbers in Hamish's exercise book. He has missed out the decimal point each time. Miss Layshun told Hamish that the 2 in each number has a value of $\frac{2}{10}$.

Write out the numbers again and put in the point so that each 2 has a value of $\frac{2}{10}$. (Column headings will help you.)

a) 6592     b) 2     c) 12

d) 54326     e) 721

To write an ordinary fraction as a decimal fraction, change first into tenths, hundredths or thousandths, then write as a decimal fraction.

For example, $2\frac{4}{5} = 2\frac{8}{10} = 2.8$.

**5**

Write the following fractions as decimal fractions.

**a)** $\frac{1}{2}$          **b)** $\frac{1}{10}$          **c)** $\frac{1}{20}$

**d)** $\frac{11}{50}$          **e)** $3\frac{27}{100}$

Change these from decimal fractions to mixed numbers in their simplest form.

For example, $6.5 = 6\frac{5}{10} \begin{smallmatrix}(\div 5) \\ (\div 5)\end{smallmatrix} = 6\frac{1}{2}$.

| f) 3.3 | g) 7.2 | h) 6.03 | i) 8.02 |
|---|---|---|---|
| j) 3.25 | k) 4.11 | l) 0.18 | m) 7.35 |
| n) 10.26 | o) 4.95 | | |

## SUMMARY

 **1**

*Speedily* see if these fractions are all of the same value. Just write *true* if they are and *false* if not.

For example, $\frac{5}{4}$, $1\frac{1}{4}$, 1.25, TRUE

a)  5.3, $\frac{53}{10}$, $5\frac{3}{10}$                    TRUE or FALSE

b)  $10\frac{1}{5}$, $\frac{51}{5}$, 10.2                    TRUE or FALSE

c)  $1\frac{17}{20}$, 1.7, $\frac{37}{20}$                    TRUE or FALSE

d)  30.5, $30\frac{1}{2}$, $\frac{61}{2}$                    TRUE or FALSE

e)  $2\frac{1}{4}$, 2.26, $\frac{9}{4}$                    TRUE or FALSE

 **2**

Write these as decimal fractions. (Remember to change the denominator into tenths, hundredths or thousandths if necessary.)

For example, $3\frac{1}{20} = 3\frac{5}{100} = 3.05$

a)  $7\frac{1}{5}$                    b)  $2\frac{1}{2}$                    c)  $14\frac{7}{100}$

d)  $1\frac{1}{2}$                    e)  $\frac{5}{50}$                    f)  $4\frac{3}{5}$ cm

110

**g)** $6\frac{9}{10}$ cm  **h)** $£6\frac{17}{20}$  **i)** $£4\frac{1}{20}$

**j)** $£3\frac{7}{100}$

 **3**

Write these as proper fractions or mixed numbers in their simplest form.

For example, $3.25 = 3\frac{25}{100} \overset{(\div 5)}{\underset{(\div 5)}{}} = 3\frac{5}{20} \overset{(\div 5)}{\underset{(\div 5)}{}} = 3\frac{1}{4}$

**a)** 6.5  **b)** 17.03  **c)** 8.12  **d)** 0.75  **e)** 4.32

**f)** 9.19  **g)** 200.01  **h)** 3.36  **i)** 5.001  **j)** 0.008

**4**

Change the first fraction of each of the following pairs into a decimal fraction, then see if it has the same value as the second fraction.

If the two fractions have the same value write them both down using an 'is equal to' sign.

For example, $\frac{5}{100}$, 0.05; $\frac{5}{100} = 0.05$

$\frac{5}{100} = 0.05$

so $\frac{7}{100} = ?$

**a)** $\frac{7}{100}$, 0.7  **b)** $\frac{1}{2}$, 0.25  **c)** $\frac{9}{100}$, 0.09

**d)** $\frac{1}{2}$, 0.5  **e)** $\frac{7}{20}$, 0.35  **f)** $\frac{4}{5}$, 0.6

111

**g)** $\frac{13}{20}$, 0.65

**h)** $\frac{1}{20}$, 0.5

**i)** $7\frac{11}{20}$, 7.54

**j)** $10\frac{9}{100}$, 10.09

 **5**

**a)** Draw a circle with radius 5 cm.

**b)** Divide the circle into 4 equal parts.

**c)** What fraction of the whole circle is each part?

**d)** Write your answer, as a fraction, in each part of the circle.

**e)** Divide one of the quarters into 5 more or less equal parts.

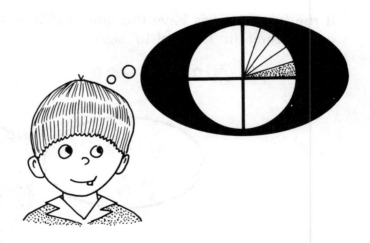

**f)** What fraction of the *whole* circle is each small part?

**g)** Write your answer to (f) as a proper fraction and as a decimal fraction.

112

# ALLSORTS

**1**

Dr Ivel, the headmaster, is planning an excursion by minibus.

*Each minibus holds 12 people plus one teacher to drive it. We want to take 30 children and 4 teachers.*

To find out how many minibuses he needed, Dr Ivel did this calculation:

$\frac{34}{13} =$     but then he spilled his coffee over it!

**a)** What was his answer?

**b)** How many mini-buses did he decide to take?

**c)** If he filled up the last minibus, how many extra passengers could he take?

**2**

Fatima and Emma have been measuring some table-tops and shelves in the school hall. They wanted to know how much crêpe paper would be needed for making Christmas decorations.

Fatima wrote down her measurements:

50 cm, 125 cm, 2 metres, 3.5 metres

**a)** Change all Fatima's measurements into metres.

**b)** Add them up.

113

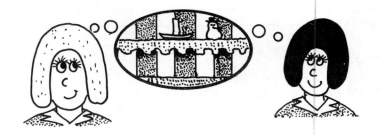

Emma wrote down her measurements:

6 metres, $2\frac{1}{2}$ metres, 0.25 m, 1 metre

**c)** Change Emma's measurements into metres and decimal fractions of a metre.

**d)** Add them up.

**e)** How many metres of paper were needed altogether?

**\*3**

Draw a shape, on squared paper, ten squares by ten squares.

**a)** Shade in $\frac{25}{100}$ of the shape in blue.

**b)** Shade in 0.25 of the shape in red.

**c)** Shade in $\frac{1}{4}$ of the shape in green.

**d)** Shade in $\frac{1}{10}$ of the shape in yellow.

**e)** Shade in 0.1 of the shape in black.

**f)** What fraction of the whole shape is unshaded?

**g)** Write your answer as a proper fraction and as a decimal fraction.

# 13. Symmetry

If a photocopier is available, copies may be taken of the diagrams* on pp.116, 117 and 119.

*Note: Copyright is waived on these diagrams only.

## PRACTICE 1 (ABC)

**1**

*Speedily* write down whether each of the following shapes is or is not symmetrical:

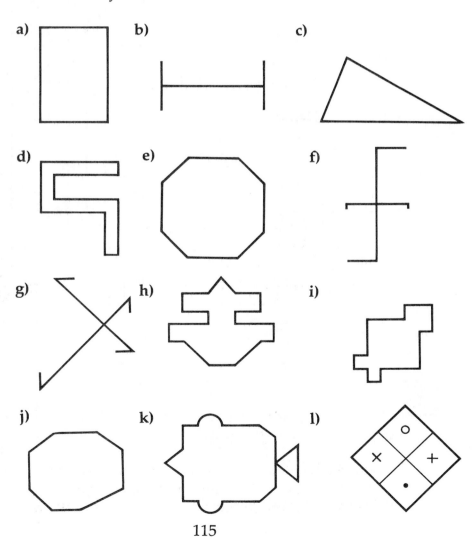

a)   b)   c)

d)   e)   f)

g)   h)   i)

j)   k)   l)

**2**

Using the squares in your book (or a photocopy) copy each of these shapes and then draw in the line of symmetry with a coloured pencil:

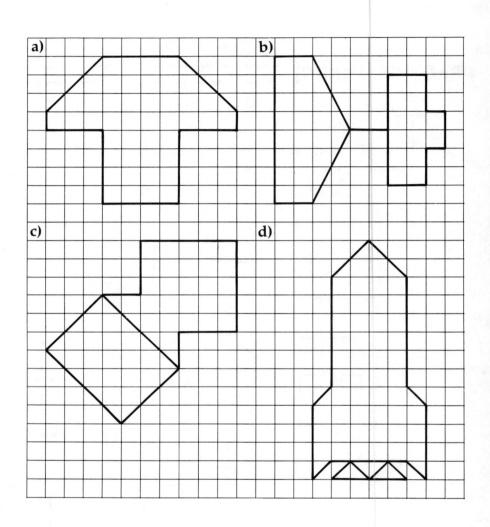

a)

b)

c)

d)

 **3**

Using the squares in your exercise book (or a photocopy) copy each of the following.

Complete the shape or pattern so that it will be symmetrical about the line of symmetry that you are given. Each time the line of symmetry is marked like this - - - - - -

116

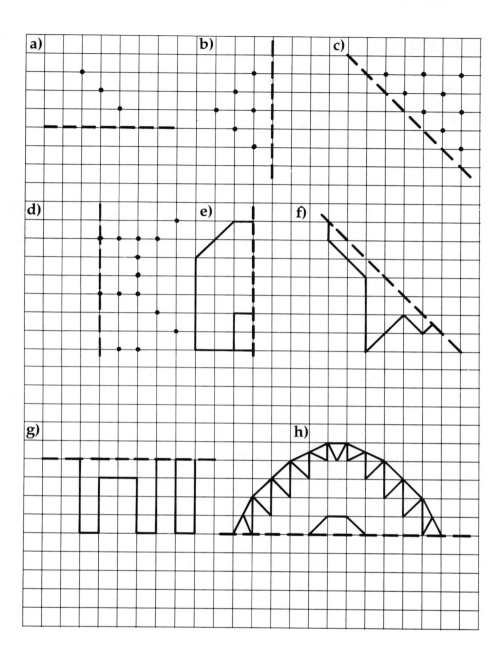

 **\*4**

**a)** Find the flags of ten countries.

**b)** Make neat drawings of them.

**c)** Mark in the line of symmetry if the flag has one. Some flags may have more than one line of symmetry. Mark in all the lines of symmetry you can find.

# ALLSORTS

 **\*1**

Follow steps (a) to (f) carefully. They will help you draw a regular hexagon.

**a)** Draw a circle to fill about half of your page.

**b)** Keeping the radius on your compasses the same, put the point of your compasses on the circumference of the circle and make one mark cutting the circumference.

**c)** Move the point of the compasses to this mark and do (b) again.

**d)** Continue round the circle until you get back to where you started.

**e)** Join each mark to the next one. You should now have a regular hexagon.

**f)** Label the points A, B, C, D, E, F, as in the diagram below.

**g)** Join point A to point D. The line AD is a line of symmetry.

**h)** Mark in 2 other similar lines of symmetry like AD.

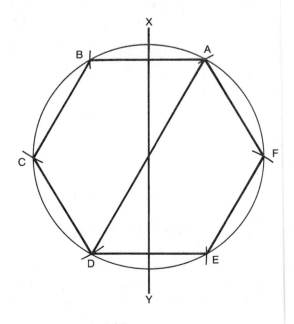

**2**

**a)** Draw another regular hexagon.

The line XY on the diagram opposite is a line of symmetry. Draw in 2 other similar lines of symmetry like XY.

**b)** How many lines of symmetry does a regular hexagon have?

**\*3**

Using a photocopy, complete each of these shapes so that they are symmetrical about the lines of symmetry given (the lines of symmetry are dotted).

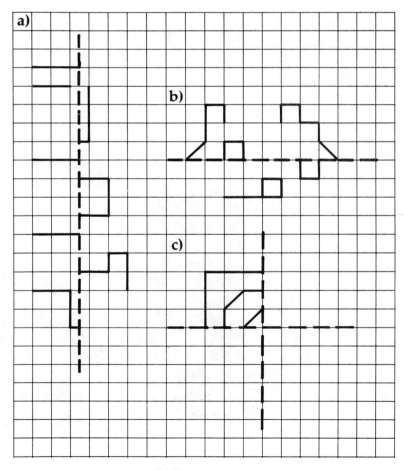

**\*4**

Dr Ivel, the headmaster, wants a new emblem for the school. He wants it to have one line of symmetry. Draw a design that might be suitable.

**\*5**

Find the 'Logos' of ten companies. Look in newspapers, magazines, on boxes and labels, etc. Try to find some that are symmetrical and some that are not. Cut them out and stick them in your book. Mark in the lines of symmetry.

# 14. Measurement iii

## PRACTICE 1 (AB)

 **1**

*Speedily* change the following 12-hour clock times to 24-hour times:

**a)** 8.0 a.m.

**b)** 9.30 p.m.

**c)** 6.15 a.m.

**d)** 11.25 p.m.

**e)** 11.25 a.m.

*Speedily* change the following 24-hour clock times to 12-hour times:

**f)** 0735

**g)** 2210

**h)** 1535

**i)** 0102

**j)** 0045

 **2**

Write the following times as 24-hour clock times:

**a)** five minutes past six p.m.

**b)** ten minutes before midnight

**c)** half past four a.m.

**d)** a quarter to eight p.m.

**e)** twenty minutes to eight a.m.

121

Write the following times as 12-hour clock times, using figures. (Don't forget a.m./p.m.)

**f)** three twenty-five in the morning

**g)** seven thirty in the evening

**h)** one minute to noon

**i)** two minutes past five in the morning

**j)** a quarter to eleven in the evening

 **3**

Look at the following digital displays, and write the times both as 24-hour times *and* 12-hour times; (a), (b) and (c) are morning; (d) and (e) are evening.

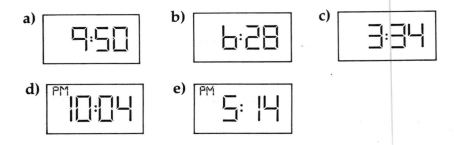

**a)** 9:50

**b)** 6:28

**c)** 3:34

**d)** PM 10:04

**e)** PM 5:14

 **4**

**a)** How many days are there in March, April, May and June altogether?

Morag, Jonathan, Hamish and Libby will all be 10 years old this year; their birthdays are shown in the table below:

| Name | 10th Birthday |
| --- | --- |
| Morag | 25th February |
| Libby | 21st August |
| Hamish | 20th November |
| Jonathan | 2nd August |

122

**b)** Write down the names of the four children in order, starting with the youngest.

**c)** If it is now October, who has not had their 10th birthday yet?

**d)** If it is now October, how many years and months old is each child? (Count part of a month as a whole month.)

**e)** How long is it from 0515 until 1137?

**f)** I am going to do a journey by train which takes 4 hours 27 minutes. If I catch the 0914 train, when will I arrive? (Write your answer as both a 12-hour clock time *and* a 24-hour clock time.)

**g)** How long is it from 1125 until 1222?

**h)** How long is it from 0843 until 0927?

**i)** How long is it from 2354 until 0039?

**\*5**

You will remember reading about Leap Years in the text; if you have forgotten, look in your note book. A Leap Year happens whenever the year's number can be divided exactly by 4.

For example $1984 \div 4 = 496$ so 1984 was a Leap Year;
$1985 \div 4 = 496\frac{1}{4}$ so 1985 was *not* a Leap Year.

The Olympic Games are always held, in a different country of the world, in a Leap Year.

Write down the last 5 Leap Years before 1984, and find out where the Olympic Games were held in each of these years.

# PRACTICE 2 (C)

 **1**

Using the timetable for your school, *speedily* write down what you would be doing at the following times:

**a)** 0910 on Monday

**b)** 0930 on Tuesday

**c)** 1015 on Wednesday

**d)** 1110 on Thursday

**e)** 1145 on Friday

**f)** 1215 on Monday

**g)** 1300 on Tuesday

**h)** 1410 on Wednesday

**i)** 1530 on Thursday

**j)** 1630 on Friday

 **2**

Here is part of a railway timetable. It shows the times when the PSM Trains leave Much Snoring and when they arrive in Dufftown.

| Train | Depart Much Snoring | Arrive Dufftown |
|-------|---------------------|-----------------|
| 1st | 0930 | 1125 |
| 2nd | 1126 | 1227 |
| 3rd | 1340 | 1445 |
| 4th | 1525 | 1650 |

**a)** Work out how long each train takes to travel from Much Snoring to Dufftown.

**b)** Which is the fastest train?

**c)** Which is the slowest train?

**d)** How much longer does this train take than the fastest train?

124

**3**

Make out another table, like the one in question 2, showing the times of the trains as 12-hour times, using a.m. and p.m.

**4**

Here is part of an old timetable showing the bus times from Much Snoring to Little Snoring-on-the-Hill:

| Much Snoring (depart) | 6.30 a.m. | 8.15 a.m. | 9.03 a.m. | 1.15 p.m. |
|---|---|---|---|---|
| Little Snoring on-the-Hill (arrive) | 7.10 a.m. | 8.55 a.m. | 9.43 a.m. | 1.55 p.m. |

Rewrite the timetable, using modern 24-hour clock times.

**5**

Write down, as accurately as you can, your time table for a typical evening at home, from the time you leave school to the time you go to bed. You could include things like: eating supper, doing homework, watching television, etc. List all the times as 24-hour clock times.

# SUMMARY

**1**

The timetable below shows the departure and arrival time of bus numbers 5, 51, 51A and 18. Use the table to work out the journey times taken by these buses.

| Bus Number | 5 | 51 | 51A | 18 |
|---|---|---|---|---|
| Depart | 1015 | 1115 | 1405 | 1607 |
| Arrive | 1055 | 1221 | 1530 | 1808 |

**2**

These were the programmes on BBC 1 TV one evening:

1620   The Perils of Penelope Pitstop

1640   Rentaghost

1705   News Round

1710   Break Point

1740   Sixty Minutes

1840   Tom & Jerry

1850   Wednesday Film: The Wrong Box

2030   The Day of the Triffids

2100   Nine O'Clock News

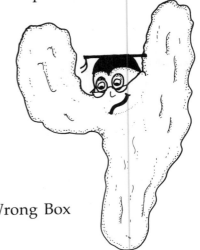

Work out how long each programme lasted.

 **3**

In the School Sports, Hamish was timed over the obstacle course. His times were:

25 m run        10 sec.

Hoops           15 sec.

Netting         20 sec.

Hollow pipe     12 sec.

Sprint finish   25 sec.

**a)** Work out his total time for the course in seconds.

**b)** Work out his total time in minutes and seconds.

**c)** If he started at 1709, at what time did he finish?

**4**

a) Look at the table below. Use it to work out the total times, in minutes and seconds, for each of these children:

|  | Tom | Fatima | Libby | Emma |
|---|---|---|---|---|
| 25 m | 10 s | 16 s | 12 s | 13 s |
| Hoops | 14 s | 23 s | 18 s | 16 s |
| Netting | 22 s | 30 s | 18 s | 21 s |
| Pipe | 13 s | 19 s | 11 s | 11 s |
| Sprint | 26 s | 32 s | 24 s | 26 s |

b) Including Hamish's time, put the children in order, starting with the fastest.

 **\*5**

Make up a bus timetable rather like the one on p.120 of the text book, with 4 stops and 5 bus journeys. Make up 5 questions about your timetable and ask a friend to answer them.

# ALLSORTS ══════════════════════════

 **1**

Tom has been asked to help make up the timetable for the Staggleton to Kinlochy bus service.

The stages of the journey take the following times:

STAGGLETON        To   LEEHAMPTON        12 mins.

LEEHAMPTON        To   THORNESVILLE      21 mins.

THORNESVILLE      To   HARVEYTOWN        15 mins.

HARVEYTOWN        To   THE SELWYN ARMS   8 mins.

THE SELWYN ARMS To   KINLOCHY           19 mins.

Copy and complete the timetable.

| Service No. | 1 | 2 | 3 |
|---|---|---|---|
| STAGGLETON | 0725 | 1020 | 1328 |
| LEEHAMPTON | | | |
| THORNESVILLE | | | |
| HARVEYTOWN | | | |
| THE SELWYN ARMS | | | |
| KINLOCHY | | | |

**2**

Last Leap Year, Libby's birthday was on Tuesday, 21st January. Hamish's birthday was on 24th May.

On which day of the week was Hamish's birthday?

**3**

This is the display on Tom's new waterproof digital watch:

$$3:28 \ {}_{!5}$$

What will be the display in 1 hour, 15 minutes and 36 seconds time?

**4**

Professor Mildew has his alarm set for 0730 exactly, so that he has plenty of time to wash, shave, dress and eat breakfast before leaving home at 0806. One morning his alarm goes off 8 minutes late. He is able to speed up his morning routine by eating one less slice of toast, and leaves home at 0808. How long does it take him to eat a slice of toast?

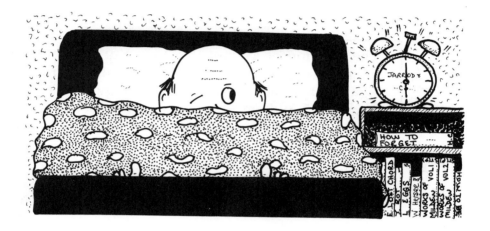

**5**

Make up a timetable for your own early morning routine, detailing as accurately as possible the time at which you start each activity.

Write your routine as a flow chart.

# 15. Starting Grids

## PRACTICE 1 (AB)

*Note:* Copies of 10 × 10 grids required.

The position of a point (8, 5) on a grid is found by taking the first number, 8, and counting across to the right that number of lines; then taking the second number, 5 and counting up that number of lines.

 **1**

*Speedily* write down the positions of the points A to H.

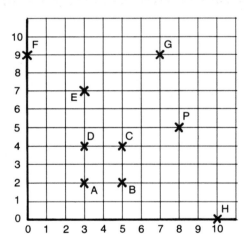

P is done for you.

P is (8, 5).

 **2**

**a)** Make up a grid like the one above, or use a photocopy, to draw the letter M. Use the points (2, 1), (2, 2), (2, 3), (2, 4) for the first line of the M, and give the positions (without using words) of the other points you use.

**b)** Starting at the point (7, 1) draw the letter E too.

130

**3**

*Battleships*

Instructions for the game of Battleships can be found in the Teacher's Guide.

Use a 10 × 10 grid.

A cruiser is made by having 3 squares shaded together in a straight line, either up or across. You know that one square is numbered (4, 3), so the whole cruiser *could* be (3, 3), (4, 3) and (5, 3).

Write down the numbers you could use to shade in 3 more cruisers.

 **4**

Use a 10 × 10 grid for this question.

Colour in the squares numbered

(2, 2), (2, 3), (2, 4), (2, 5), (2, 6), (2, 7),

(5, 1), (5, 2), (5, 3), (5, 6), (5, 7),

(8, 5), (8, 6), (8, 7), (8, 8), (8, 9), (8, 10).

These are dangerous minefields and you must not use these squares.

Start half way up the left-hand side of the grid at (1, 5) and see how many moves (across or up only) you need to get half way up the right-hand side (10, 5).

131

***5**

Put a plan of your classroom and its desks on a 10 × 10 grid. You can fill in a whole square for each desk.

Put in the teacher's desk or table too. Make it as accurate as you can.

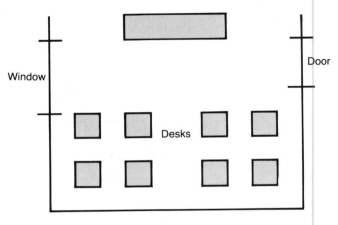

# Practice 2 (C)

*Note:* Copies of 10 × 10 grids required.

 **1**

*Speedily* join up the following points on a 6 × 6 grid to make a letter .

**a)** (2, 1) to (2, 2) to (2, 3) to (3, 2) to (4, 1) to (4, 2) to (4, 3).

**b)** (5, 1) to (5, 2) to (5, 3) to (6, 3) to (6, 2) to (5, 2).

 **2**

Emma and Tom are using paving slabs, which are 1 m square, for a grid. Emma is at the point (4, 7). Tom is at (8, 7).

**a)** How far apart are Emma and Tom?

**b)** Hamish is at (8, 4). How far away from Tom is he?

**c)** Draw these positions on a grid and measure how far Hamish is from Emma. It's a whole number.

**3**

*Battleships*

A submarine is made by shading 2 squares. They have to be next to one another, but on a diagonal. So a submarine could be (3, 1), (4, 2).

Draw a grid and shade these two squares.

If one part of another submarine is at (5, 5), write down the four other squares where the rest of it could be.

 **4**

Use this machine which takes away 2 from a number:

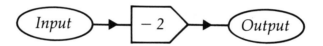

**a)** Input the numbers 2, 3, 4, 5, 6 and 10; and write down the outputs in a table like this:

| INPUT | −2 | OUTPUT |
|-------|-----|--------|
| 2 | | |
| 3 | | |
| 4 | | |
| . | | |
| . | | |
| . | | |

Use each input as the *first* number and each output as the *second* number to plot 6 points, then join them up.

**b)** Are they in a straight line?

**5**

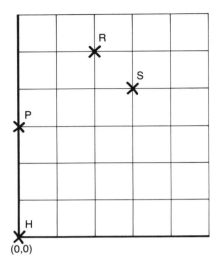

Emma's home is at H, (0, 0) as a point.

There are km squares for the grid, but you can draw cm squares on a photocopy of a 10 × 10 square.

She usually walks to school, going straight to the Post Office P at (0, 3) and then straight to the school S at (3, 4).

She wonders if it would be quicker to walk via the Railway Station R at (2, 5) instead of via P.

**a)** Draw Emma's routes carefully on the grid by joining up the points.

**b)** Measure HP, PS, HR, and RS and work out which route is quicker.

# SUMMARY

*Note:* Copies of 10 × 10 grids required.

**1**

*Speedily* write down the positions of the points J to Q.

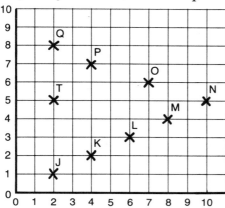

T is done for you.

T is (2, 5).

**2**

**a)** Use a grid like the one above, or use a photocopy, and make the letter X. Start at the point (3, 1).

**b)** Now make the letter Y, starting at the point (7, 1).

**3**

Join up the following points and see what you get!

**a)** (2, 3) to (2, 5) to (3, 5) to (3, 4) to (2, 4).

**b)** (4, 3) to (5, 3) to (5, 4) to (4, 4) to (4, 5) to (5, 5).

**c)** (6, 3) to (6, 5) to (7, 4) to (8, 5) to (8, 3).

**4**

Miss Layshun is at the point (10, 5). Libby's desk is at (5, 5) and Fatima's at (6, 8).

Draw these on a grid, marking the points carefully.

The children argue about who is nearer to Miss Layshun. Measure the distances on your grid and decide.

5

You will need to draw two copies of the number square below, making them larger (each small square should have 1 cm sides).

a) Colour red all the numbers which are in the 7 times table, taken on to 100. There are six *rows* where only one square is coloured, but four rows where two squares are coloured.

Give the positions of the coloured squares in the rows where only one is coloured. The second one is 4 along, 9 up.

Then give the positions of the coloured squares in the columns where only one square in the column is coloured.

b) Do the same for numbers in the 6 times table—taken on to 100.

| 10 | 1 | 2 | 3 | 4 | 5 | 6 | 7 | 8 | 9 | 10 |
|---|---|---|---|---|---|---|---|---|---|---|
| 9 | 11 | 12 | 13 | 14 | 15 | 16 | 17 | 18 | 19 | 20 |
| 8 | 21 | 22 | 23 | 24 | 23 | 26 | 27 | 28 | 29 | 30 |
| 7 | 31 | 32 | 33 | 34 | 35 | 36 | 37 | 38 | 39 | 40 |
| 6 | 41 | 42 | 43 | 44 | 45 | 46 | 47 | 48 | 49 | 50 |
| 5 | 51 | 52 | 53 | 54 | 55 | 56 | 57 | 58 | 59 | 60 |
| 4 | 61 | 62 | 63 | 64 | 65 | 66 | 67 | 68 | 69 | 70 |
| 3 | 71 | 72 | 73 | 74 | 75 | 76 | 77 | 78 | 79 | 80 |
| 2 | 81 | 82 | 83 | 84 | 85 | 86 | 87 | 88 | 89 | 90 |
| 1 | 91 | 92 | 93 | 94 | 95 | 96 | 97 | 98 | 99 | 100 |
|  | 1 | 2 | 3 | 4 | 5 | 6 | 7 | 8 | 9 | 10 |

# ALLSORTS

1

Look at this × 3 machine.

| In | ×3 | Out |
|---|---|---|
| 3 | → | 9 |
| 4 | → | 12 |
| . |  | . |

136

Now put it with a − 8 machine as in the second table.

| | ×3 | | −8 | |
|---|---|---|---|---|
| 3 | → | 9 | → | 1 |
| 4 | → | 12 | → | . |
| 5 | → | . | → | . |
| 6 | → | . | → | . |
| 7 | → | . | | . |

a) Complete the second table.

b) Use the *first* number and the *last* as the two parts of a point (the first one is worked out for you and is (3, 1)) and put these points on a 10 × 10 grid. One won't fit on!

Join them up—you'll soon see if one is wrong.

 **\*2**

a) Look at a grid on an Ordnance Survey map. The numbered lines *across* are 1 km apart, so are the ones that go up.

Find the nearest town or city to your school and work out which square it is in.

b) Choose a seaside resort and find out which square it is in.

(For example, × is in square (13, 24).)

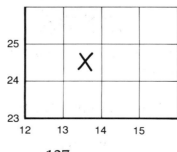

**c)** If a point is due North of (17, 3) what must its first number be?

**d)** What if it is due South?

## 3

*Battleships*
**a)** You need a 10 × 10 grid. If a submarine can be *any* pair of squares next door to one another, including the diagonals, how many possible squares are there to guess from if you know one part of a submarine is at (3, 3)?

Write down the squares that you could guess.

**b)** Play a simple game of battleships on a 10 × 10 grid and see how long it takes to finish.

Then make a 20 × 20 grid for yourself (you can halve each square of a 10 × 10) and see how long it takes to finish a game now!

How many squares are there on a 20 × 20 grid?

## *4

Find out how grid positions are used:

**a)** for seats in a theatre (they probably use letters *and* numbers, but the idea is the same);

**b)** for the roads in New York City (notice that Broadway is 'different');

**c)** on the National Grid for the whole of the UK;

**d)** for any other purpose.

# 16. Statistics ii

## PRACTICE 1 (AB)

If a whole pie chart represents 15 people, the angle of the sector representing one person is:

$$\frac{360° \ (÷ 5)}{15 \ (÷ 5)} = \frac{72°}{3} = \frac{24°}{1} = 24°$$

**1**

*Speedily* work out the angle of the sector representing *one* person for each of these totals:

a) 36        b) 10        c) 18

d) 60        e) 90        f) 4

**2**

*Speedily* find the *averages* of the following:

a) 5 cm, 10 cm, 15 cm.

b) 3 kg, 4 kg, 7 kg, 2 kg.

c) 8 minutes, 10 minutes, 18 minutes.

d) 4, 10, 5, 6, 20.

e) 12 mm, 15 mm, 18 mm.

f) 6p, 18p, 6p.

**3**

**Pie Chart showing Holidays taken by 18 Pupils in Form 4**

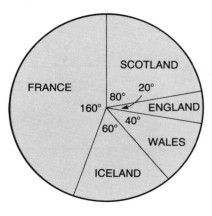

a) What angle of sector represents each pupil?

How many pupils spent their holiday in:

**b)** Wales          **c)** Iceland          **d)** France?

 **4**

**Pie Chart showing how Tom spent £3.60 given to him by his Grannie**

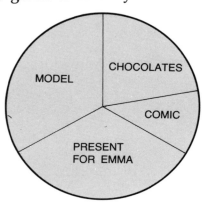

Tom has forgotten to label the angles of the sectors, but you can measure them!

a) What angle of sector represents each *penny* spent by Tom?

How much did Tom spend on:

**b)** the model          **c)** chocolates          **d)** the present for Emma?

### *5

Fatima has baked 4 cakes and their masses are:

960 g, 810 g, 930 g, 780 g.

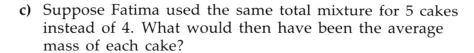

What is:

**a)** the total mass?

**b)** the average mass?

**c)** Suppose Fatima used the same total mixture for 5 cakes instead of 4. What would then have been the average mass of each cake?

# PRACTICE 2 (CD)

**1**

*Speedily* use this table of data to write down the answers to the questions which follow:

| Model | Mass (g) | Length (cm) | Width (cm) | Height (cm) |
|---|---|---|---|---|
| A | 150 | 20 | 2 | 7 |
| B | 200 | 18 | 11 | 9 |
| C | 120 | 16 | 13 | 6 |
| D | 180 | 19 | 10 | 10 |

Which model has the greatest:

**a)** mass  **b)** length
**c)** width  **d)** height?

**e)** Which model has a mass of less than 160 g and is less than 13 cm wide?

 **2**

**a)** *Speedily* work out the average height, using the bar chart below.

**b)** Calculate the average height of the models using the flow chart method from 'Statistics ii'; Book B.

**Bar Chart showing Heights of 4 Models in question 1**

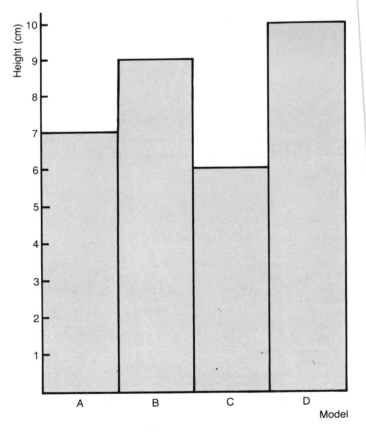

**3**

Look at the table below. Write down the names of the children:

**a)** with blue eyes;

**b)** with less than 2 fillings;

**c)** with birthdays in June;

**d)** with a mass of *over* 30 kg;

**e)** who are taller than Jean-Pierre.

Look at the column which tells you the children's heights.

**f)** Write down the name of anyone who is 132 cm or more.

**g)** Which child has a birthday in August *and* a mass of less than 40 kg?

| | Mass (kg) | Height (cm) | Eye colour | Birthday | Number of tooth fillings |
|---|---|---|---|---|---|
| Tom | 32 | 132 | Blue | June | 1 |
| Hamish | 30 | 128 | Brown | August | 3 |
| Emma | 28 | 129 | Brown | September | 0 |
| Morag | 29 | 125 | Blue | January | 2 |
| Jean-Pierre | 31 | 130 | Blue | March | 1 |
| Libby | 34 | 133 | Green | February | 2 |
| Fatima | 45 | 131 | Hazel | August | 5 |
| Jonathan | 30 | 129 | Blue | November | 0 |

**4**

Here is a bar chart showing the heights of the pupils, from the data in question 3. T stands for Tom, H for Hamish and so on.

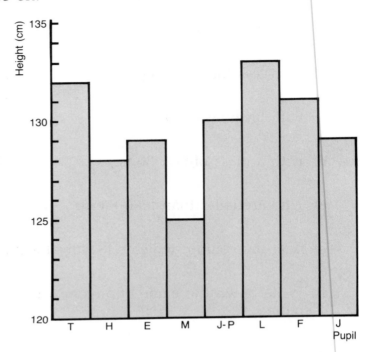

a) Why do you think that the bar chart does not start at zero on the height axis?

b) Is Libby *really* more than *twice* as tall as Morag?

c) By looking at the bar chart, try to find the average height. Give your answer to the nearest whole number.

d) Find the average height by the flow chart method as a check.
(Use a calculator, if your teacher will let you.)
Do your answers agree?

 **\*5**

a) Prepare a data table of your own.
This could be for example *'pencils in my case'* (length, colour, make, etc.) or *'stamps in my collection'* (country, colour, value, etc.).

b) Write down a few questions for a friend to answer.

# SUMMARY

 **1** Pie Chart showing how the 24 hours of Tom's Saturday are spent

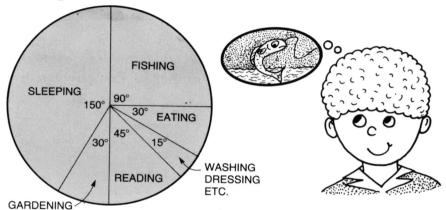

**a)** How many degrees represent one hour?

How many hours are spent:

**b)** sleeping          **c)** eating?

What *fraction* of his time is spent:

**d)** reading          **e)** fishing?

 **2**

Tom and 4 of his friends compare their pocket money:

Emma 50p, Tom £1.00, Libby 60p, Hamish 75p, Morag 80p.

What is the average pocket money?

 **3**

Consider a survey involving 20 people.

**a)** What will be the angle of sector representing 1 person on a pie chart?

145

**b)** What will be the angle of sector representing a group of 4 people?

**c)** If one sector has an angle of 144°, how many people will it represent?

 **4**

**Bar Chart showing Number of Pens owned by Children**

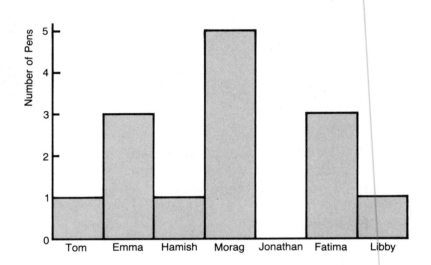

How many pens are owned by:

**a)** Tom          **b)** Morag          **c)** Jonathan?

**d)** How many pens are there altogether?

**e)** How many children are included in the survey?

**f)** Looking at the bar chart, share out the pens fairly. (Clearly Morag could give a few to Jonathan!) How many would the children have each?

**g)** What is the average number of pens for one pupil?

 **\*5**

Draw a pie chart, similar to question 1, for your *own* day!

# ALLSORTS

**1**

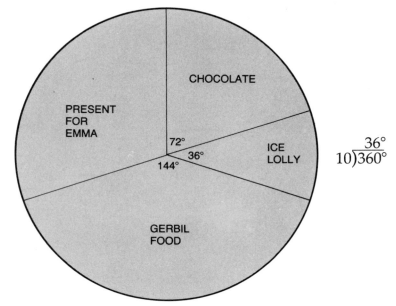

CHOCOLATE

PRESENT
FOR
EMMA

72°

36°

144°

ICE
LOLLY

GERBIL
FOOD

$$\begin{array}{r} 36° \\ 10\overline{)360°} \end{array}$$

Tom has started to draw a pie chart showing how he spent his £1.00 pocket money.

His ice lolly cost 10p.

How much did he spend on the present for Emma?

**2**

Emma's Uncle Sam has sent her a box of pieces of meteorite from the large crater in Arizona.

Altogether there are 5 pieces and their average mass is 480 g.

What is the total mass of the package? (Ignore the mass of the packing materials!)

147

**3**

In Science, Libby has been learning that about $\frac{4}{5}$ of air is a gas called *nitrogen*.

Another gas, *oxygen*, makes up almost all of the rest!

She has started to draw a pie chart.

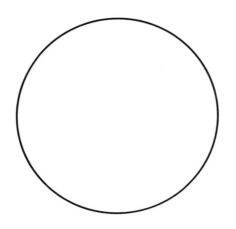

$$5)\overline{\phantom{0}360°}^{\,72°}$$

Nitrogen   4 × 72° =
Oxygen   1 × 72° =

Finish it off for her.

 **4**

Odif, Dr Ivel's dog, likes variety in his food, although he is not very clever. Dr Ivel has bought a 10-day supply of food for him.

　8 cans Economy Doggynosh
　2 cans Wuffalot
　3 cans Prawn Cocktail flavour Bongs
　4 cans Pussycat flavour Bongs
　2 cans Gerbil flavour Bongs

and as a special treat

　1 can Postman flavour Bongs.

**a)** Represent this as a bar chart.

**b)** Using the bar chart, find the average number of cans of each type of food.

**c)** *Calculate* the average number of cans of each type of food.

**\*5**

Draw a pie chart to represent the data in question 4.